Targeting N

CALCULATIONS

Paul Broadbent

Rob Kearsley Bullen

 LONGMAN

Pearson Education Limited,
Edinburgh Gate, Harlow
Essex CM20 2JE, England
and Associated Companies throughout the World.

First published 1998
Second impression 2000

ISBN 0 582 31972 2

Printed in Singapore (PH)

The publisher's policy is to use paper manufactured from sustainable forests.

About Targeting Number

Targeting Number is a supplementary resource which aims to address the difficulties in number skills commonly experienced by pupils starting secondary mathematics. The resource is comprised of a *Teacher's Guide* and two pupil's books entitled *Calculations* and *The Number System*.

The Teacher's Guide provides 90 suggested lesson plans, each of which centres around a class activity. The plans are divided into 9 sections of 10 lessons, with each section covering a particular area of Number.

Targeting Number is designed for use along side any course or scheme of work: by using sets of the pupils books with different classes and copying the necessary lesson material from the Teacher's Guide, the resource can be used whenever teachers wish to dedicate a lesson to the mastery of specific number skills and concepts.

About this book

Calculations provides practice for lessons from sections 1 to 5 which cover work on the four operations. For each lesson there are two pupil's book pages of carefully graded exercises which reinforce and follow on from the skills and concepts learnt through the main lesson activity. This material can be used during the lesson or set as homework.

Answers to all exercises can are found in the Teacher's Guide.

Acknowledgements

The authors and Publisher would like to thank the following for their critical assessment of the *Targeting Number* material, their helpful comments and valuable suggestions.

Christine Gordon, Head of Mathematics, Harrytown School, Romiley, Stockport.
John Derbyshire, Director After School Project, Nottingham.
Wendy Fortescue-Hubbard, research student University of Plymouth, Head of Mathematics, Dartmouth Community College.
Shaun Shore, Bishop Challoner School, Birmingham.
Julia Whitburn, Senior Research Officer, National Institute of Economic and Social Research.

CONTENTS

Calculations: The Four Operations

Addition 1

Addition bonds to 20

Keywords ● sum ● total ● add ● addition ● plus ● result ● addition bonds ● more than

A

Here are some groups of three numbers. Put signs in between the numbers so that they make a correct sum. You can have one "+" and one "=". You can use the numbers in any order. Warning! One of them is a trick question – can you find it?

1. 3 4 1
2. 2 4 2
3. 3 9 6
4. 5 2 3

5. 5 5 10
6. 8 1 7
7. 1 6 5
8. 4 8 5

9. 9 2 7
10. 3 7 4
11. 3 7 10
12. 2 8 6

B

Write down **all** the pairs of numbers whose sum is 10.
How can you be sure you've found them all?

C

Copy and complete these additions.

1. $2 + 9 =$
2. $9 + 2 =$
3. $7 + 5 =$
4. $5 + 7 =$

5. $8 + 6 =$
6. $6 + 8 =$
7. $9 + 7 =$
8. $7 + 9 =$

9. $4 + 8 =$
10. $8 + 4 =$
11. $3 + 9 =$
12. $9 + 3 =$

D

Write down **all** the pairs of numbers that add up to 20.
How can you be sure you've found them all?

E

Work out what each question means, then write out the sum and work out the answer. When you have found the answer, write it in **words**.

1. Find the sum of six and seven.
2. What number is eight more than five?
3. Eight is added to eight. What is the total?
4. What do you get if you add nine and nine?
5. What is the sum of four and seven?

6. Work out five plus nine.
7. Find the total if you add six and six.
8. What is eleven added to three?
9. Add together twelve and four.
10. What is the sum of eight and nine?

F

Each function machine has five numbers that are fed into it. Copy the table, then work out the output numbers and fill in the last column.

	Input numbers	Machine	Output numbers
1.	1, 2, 3, 4, 5	+ 6	
2.	6, 7, 8, 9, 10	+ 9	
3.	2, 4, 6, 8, 10	+ 5	
4.	1, 3, 5, 7, 9	+ 10	
5.	15, 12, 9, 6, 3	+ 4	
6.	16, 12, 8, 4, 0	+ 3	

Think for yourself…

Addition Patterns

In the input and output numbers from the machines in section **F**, there are lots of patterns.

(a) Look carefully at the numbers and write down any patterns you find.
(b) Carry on each pattern with five more numbers. They must use the same rules. Do you notice anything about the patterns in the input and output for each machine?
(c) Now make up some of your own. You need a set of input numbers with a rule, and an addition machine like the ones in section **F**.
(d) You could make some of your results from (c) into questions for your neighbour. He or she has to work out the output numbers and write down what the patterns are.

Missing numbers

Keywords ● sum ● total ● add ● addition ● plus ● result ● more than

A

Each of these has a number missing. Copy and complete the sum.

1. 3 + ? = 11	**5.** 6 + ? = 18	**9.** ? + 9 = 18
2. 14 + ? = 16	**6.** ? + 4 = 20	**10.** ? + 14 = 19
3. 10 + ? = 15	**7.** ? + 11 = 17	**11.** 8 + 8 = ?
4. 9 + ? = 14	**8.** ? + 7 = 13	**12.** 13 + ? = 13

B

Work out the answers to these.

1. 2 + 3 + 4	**5.** 8 + 2 + 5	**9.** 14 + 2 + 3
2. 4 + 5 + 6	**6.** 4 + 4 + 4	**10.** 5 + 11 + 1
3. 5 + 8 + 1	**7.** 9 + 2 + 3	**11.** 6 + 2 + 10
4. 6 + 3 + 3	**8.** 5 + 6 + 7	**12.** 1 + 1 + 11

C

Each pair of function machines has five numbers that are fed in. Copy the table, then work out the missing numbers and fill in the blank columns.

	Input numbers	1st Machine	Middle numbers	2nd Machine	Output numbers
1.	1, 2, 3, 4, 5	+ 4		+ 3	
2.	5, 6, 7, 8, 9	+ 9		+ 1	
3.	2, 4, 6, 8, 10	+ 5		+ 5	
4.	0, 3, 6, 9, 12	+ 2		+ 6	
5.	6, 5, 4, 3, 2	+ 8		+ 5	
6.	11, 9, 7, 5, 3	+ 2		+ 7	

D

Each of these has a number missing. Copy and complete the sum.

1. $2 + 6 + ? = 11$

2. $3 + 7 + ? = 15$

3. $3 + 6 + ? = 19$

4. $5 + 8 + ? = 14$

5. $? + 1 + 6 = 9$

6. $? + 5 + 12 = 18$

7. $? + 6 + 7 = 16$

8. $? + 2 + 4 = 11$

9. $2 + ? + 2 = 7$

10. $8 + ? + 4 = 17$

11. $3 + ? + 6 = 19$

12. $5 + ? + 5 = 15$

E

Each of these has **two** numbers missing.
Find *at least* three different ways of completing each one.

1. $5 + ? + ? = 15$

2. $7 + ? + ? = 13$

3. $? + ? + 3 = 12$

4. $? + 6 + ? = 16$

5. $? + 11 + ? = 19$

Think for yourself ...

Number Triangles

Here are two number triangles. They gave the same number in the middle. Look at them and see if you can figure out how they work.

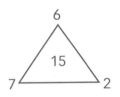
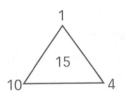

These both have 6 in the middle

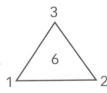
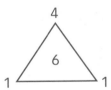

Can you find any more triangles with 6 in the middle?
How can you be sure you've found them all?

Choose a different number for the middle of the triangle.
How many triangles can you find? Is this more, or less than you got for "6"?
Why do you think this is?

Addition 3

Tens bonds

Keywords ● sum ● total ● add ● addition ● plus ● result ● more than ● multiply

A

Here are some groups of three numbers. Put signs in between the numbers so that they make a correct sum. You can have one "+" and one "=". You can use the numbers in any order. Warning! One of them is a trick question – can you find it?

1.	20	40	60	**5.**	30	40	70	**9.**	40	30	70
2.	10	70	80	**6.**	50	90	40	**10.**	20	30	30
3.	40	20	20	**7.**	60	80	20	**11.**	90	20	70
4.	60	50	10	**8.**	80	90	10	**12.**	40	60	20

B

Write down **all** the pairs of numbers whose sum is 100. (It's not as bad as it sounds – you only need to use multiples of 10). How can you be sure you've found them all?

C

Use the **Number lines** sheet for this section. Show the answers with an arrow. Here's an example:

13 + 10 = ?

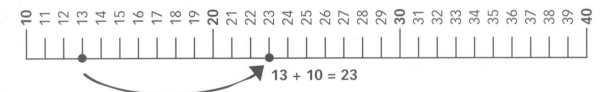

13 + 10 = 23

1.	24 + 10 = ?	**6.**	45 + 20 = ?
2.	37 + 10 = ?	**7.**	86 + 10 = ?
3.	51 + 10 = ?	**8.**	18 + 20 = ?
4.	24 + 20 = ?	**9.**	73 + 10 = ?
5.	72 + 20 = ?	**10.**	33 + 20 = ?

Learning Objectives
To use the addition bonds to calculate the addition of multiples of ten
To be able to add any multiple of ten to a TU number

D

Find the missing number that makes each line true.

1.	31 + ? = 41	**5.**	45 + ? = 75	**9.**	? + 52 = 72
2.	21 + ? = 41	**6.**	39 + ? = 89	**10.**	? + 29 = 69
3.	17 + ? = 37	**7.**	78 + ? = 88	**11.**	? + 41 = 91
4.	17 + ? = 47	**8.**	13 + ? = 83	**12.**	15 + ? = 95

E

Each function machine has five numbers that are fed into it.
Copy the table, then work out the output numbers and fill in the last column.

	Input numbers	Machine	Output numbers
1.	3, 4, 5, 6, 7	+ 10	
2.	6, 7, 8, 9, 10	+ 20	
3.	22, 24, 26, 28, 30	+ 50	
4.	1, 5, 9, 13, 17	+ 80	
5.	53, 48, 43, 38, 33	+ 30	
6.	35, 30, 26, 23, 21	+ 60	

Think for yourself …

Ten-splits

Pick any number between 10 and 100.

Write down all the ways you can find of splitting this number up using two-digit numbers and multiples of 10 (for example, 23 splits up in two ways: 10 + 13 and also 20 + 3).

Try this out with different numbers. Which one has the most splits? Which one has the least? Why?

Is there a rule that lets you know how many splits a number will have, without trying to write them all down?

Addition 4

Tens and units

Keywords ● sum ● total ● add

A

For each of these, write a sum in figures, then write the answer in words.

1. ten plus six
2. eight plus ten
3. eight plus thirty
4. forty plus three
5. seventy plus one
6. nine plus twenty
7. six plus fifty
8. eight plus eighty
9. ninety plus two
10. forty plus four
11. one plus sixty
12. Write one like this that will give an answer equal to your age.

B

Find the missing numbers.

1. $30 + ? = 34$
2. $? + 40 = 41$
3. $20 + ? = 29$
4. $50 + ? = 55$
5. $? + 10 = 13$
6. $80 + ? = 89$
7. $? + 6 = 46$
8. $7 + ? = 77$
9. $? + 8 = 58$
10. $? + 3 = 23$
11. $4 + ? = 94$
12. $? + 2 = 62$

C

Work out the answers to these.

1. $23 + 4$
2. $12 + 7$
3. $53 + 1$
4. $34 + 5$
5. $73 + 3$
6. $88 + 1$
7. $63 + 5$
8. $92 + 6$
9. $44 + 4$
10. $37 + 2$

D

Each function machine has five numbers that are fed into it. Copy the table, then work out the output numbers and fill in the last column.

	Input numbers	Machine	Output numbers
1.	23, 24, 25, 26, 27	+ 2	
2.	46, 47, 48, 49, 50	+ 4	
3.	22, 24, 26, 28, 30	+ 5	
4.	10, 14, 18, 22, 26	+ 9	
5.	93, 88, 83, 78, 73	+ 6	
6.	25, 20, 16, 13, 11	+ 7	

E

Work out what each question means, then write out the sum and work out the answer. When you have found the answer, write it in **words**.

1. Find the sum of sixty-one and seven.
2. What number is eight more than fifty-eight?
3. Eight is added to eighty-four. What is the total?
4. What do you get if you add forty-two and nine?
5. What is the sum of fourteen and seven?
6. Work out thirty-nine plus nine.
7. Find the total if you add six and sixty-six.
8. What is seventy-three added to three?
9. Add together twenty-six and four.
10. What is the sum of ninety-eight and three?

F

Find the missing numbers.

1. $35 + ? = 39$
2. $? + 45 = 51$
3. $22 + ? = 30$
4. $57 + ? = 65$
5. $? + 15 = 23$
6. $85 + ? = 92$
7. $? + 6 = 52$
8. $7 + ? = 81$
9. $? + 8 = 37$
10. $? + 3 = 20$
11. $4 + ? = 93$
12. $? + 2 = 61$

Think for yourself ...

Offspring

Take any two-digit number (say, 23). Use the two digits as separate numbers (2 and 3) and add these back on to the original number:

$23 + 2 + 3 = 28$.

So the "offspring" of 23 is 28, and the "parent" of 28 is 23. The "offspring" of 61 would be 68.

(a) What is the smallest two-digit "parent" with a three-digit "offspring"?
(b) Every two-digit number has an "offspring", but are there any numbers that don't have "parents"? Is there a pattern to your answers?
(c) What happens if you follow a number's "family tree", looking at each new "generation"?
(d) Is there a good diagram that could illustrate your findings?
(e) What would happen if you used larger numbers?

Addition 5

Adding two-digit numbers

Keywords ● sum ● total ● add

A

Each pair of function machines has three numbers that are fed in. Copy the table, then work out the missing numbers and fill in the blank columns.

	Input numbers	1st Machine	Middle numbers	2nd Machine	Output numbers
1.	3, 4, 5	+ 10		+ 4	
2.	10, 12, 14	+ 20		+ 6	
3.	34, 33, 32	+ 50		+ 5	
4.	21, 24, 27	+ 40		+ 2	
5.	69, 65, 61	+ 30		+ 1	
6.	14, 12, 10	+ 70		+ 4	

Now, for each part, draw a **single** function machine that will do the same job as the two machines together.

B

Do these **in your head**. You can split the work up into two steps, as in section A.

1. 23 + 15
2. 45 + 22
3. 67 + 31
4. 16 + 53
5. 82 + 14
6. 61 + 26
7. 24 + 24
8. 75 + 14
9. 38 + 41
10. 43 + 45
11. 72 + 25
12. 43 + 36

C

Find the missing numbers.

1. 21 + ? = 34
2. ? + 43 = 64
3. 23 + ? = 49
4. 56 + ? = 78
5. ? + 15 = 47
6. 35 + ? = 89
7. ? + 67 = 99
8. 53 + ? = 77
9. ? + 18 = 59
10. ? + 23 = 46
11. 41 + ? = 94
12. ? + 25 = 68

D

This diagram shows a pair of numbers that add up to make 40.

$19 \rightarrow (40) \leftarrow 21$

1. Draw four more diagrams like this to show pairs of numbers that add up to make 40.

For each of these parts, draw five diagrams like the ones above.

2.
$\rightarrow (45) \leftarrow$

3.
$\rightarrow (28) \leftarrow$

4.
$\rightarrow (69) \leftarrow$

5.
$\rightarrow (82) \leftarrow$

E

Use any method you can to answer these.

1. 32 + 58
2. 54 + 26
3. 28 + 27
4. 46 + 46

5. 73 + 19
6. 38 + 44
7. 15 + 17
8. 63 + 28

9. 49 + 29
10. 23 + 58
11. 13 + 56 + 24
12. 37 + 27 + 17

F

What's different about these? Answer them to find out.

1. 62 + 55
2. 31 + 94

3. 46 + 56
4. 78 + 25

5. 65 + 77
6. 88 + 85

Think for yourself ...

Reversing

Pick any two-digit number (suppose you pick 23). Reverse the digits (you now have 32). Add the reversed number to the original (23 + 32 = 55). Find other numbers that give 55 in this way. What do they have in common? How many are there? How can you be sure you've found them all?

Try a different starting number. **If the total gets bigger than 100, try something smaller.** Find the other numbers that give the same total as this one. Are there more or less than the "55"s? Why do you think that is?

What happens if you try this with a number whose total is bigger than 100?

Into the hundreds

Keywords ● sum ● total ● add ● column ● zero

A

Do these in your head.

Here's an example. To work out 250 + 70, do 25 + 7 = 32, then add a zero (0) to the end: 320!

1. 250 + 40	**4.** 390 + 50	**7.** 270 + 710	**10.** 180 + 170
2. 180 + 60	**5.** 160 + 120	**8.** 540 + 300	**11.** 630 + 190
3. 660 + 70	**6.** 420 + 350	**9.** 260 + 360	**12.** 350 + 470

B

Do these mentally, then check your answers by setting out the sums in columns.

1. 142 + ? = 148	**4.** 656 + ? = 664	**7.** 755 + ? = 815	**10.** 762 + ? = 962
2. 451 + ? = 459	**5.** 256 + ? = 286	**8.** 582 + ? = 622	**11.** 697 + ? = 1097
3. 347 + ? = 350	**6.** 844 + ? = 864	**9.** 435 + ? = 735	**12.** 733 + ? = 1233

C

Work out the answers to these.

1. 242 + 24	**4.** 548 + 33	**7.** 647 + 52	**10.** 163 + 58
2. 356 + 32	**5.** 661 + 29	**8.** 833 + 91	**11.** 445 + 75
3. 715 + 63	**6.** 947 + 45	**9.** 284 + 82	**12.** 967 + 84

D

Set these out in columns, then answer them.

1. 542 + 233	**5.** 461 + 429	**9.** 384 + 382	**13.** 676 + 511
2. 456 + 241	**6.** 847 + 145	**10.** 163 + 358	**14.** 432 + 584
3. 715 + 174	**7.** 247 + 552	**11.** 745 + 175	**15.** 888 + 777
4. 648 + 316	**8.** 433 + 391	**12.** 467 + 484	

Learning Objectives
To be able to use a written method for adding numbers greater than 100
To develop estimation skills for calculating approximate answers

E

The table shows the distance in kilometres between certain cities in the UK.

TO \ FROM	Aberdeen	Cambridge	Cardiff	Exeter	Liverpool	London	York
Aberdeen		742	792	911	538	806	497
Cambridge	742		290	351	296	84	253
Cardiff	792	290		192	264	249	389
Exeter	911	351	192		385	275	467
Liverpool	538	296	264	385		330	158
London	806	84	249	275	330		315
York	497	253	389	467	158	315	

Work out the distance a lorry would have to travel on each of the journeys given here.
Check your answers for numbers 1 to 7 – they should work out slightly longer than the direct journey.

1. London to York, via Cambridge.
2. Exeter to London, via Cardiff.
3. Liverpool to London, via Cambridge.
4. Liverpool to Exeter, via Cardiff.
5. York to Cardiff, via Liverpool.
6. London to Aberdeen, via Cambridge and York.
7. Aberdeen to Exeter, via York, Liverpool and Cardiff.
8. A circular route, starting and finishing at London, visiting Cardiff, Liverpool, York and Cambridge.

Think for yourself...

Five Fives (I)

(a) Using five "5"s, how many different numbers can you make? You can use any number of "5"s (as long as it's not more than 5) and any number of "+" signs.

Here are two examples to start you off: $5 + 5 = 10$, $55 + 5 = 60$.

(b) What can you make with four "4"s?
(c) What about six "6"s?
(d) Try some other numbers.
(e) Try mixing up – which makes more numbers, seven "4"s or four "7"s? Which makes the *biggest* number?

Addition 7

Four digits

Keywords ● sum ● total ● add ● thousand ● digit ● column

A

Work these out in your head.

1. 2361 + 2000
2. 5224 + 60
3. 800 + 1142
4. 40 + 6355
5. 9294 + 600
6. 7000 + 2881
7. 6275 + 80
8. 8332 + 900
9. 400 + 1611
10. 60 + 6666

B

You should be able to work these out in your head, but if not, set them out in columns.

1. 4136 + 1200
2. 5466 + 23
3. 430 + 2145
4. 1600 + 1453
5. 3343 + 180
6. 56 + 9015
7. 820 + 2333
8. 4848 + 390
9. 6153 + 58
10. 4400 + 5604

C

These need to be set out in columns.

1. 6142 + 1321
2. 5006 + 833
3. 6303 + 3127
4. 746 + 5116
5. 9164 + 442
6. 4490 + 1353
7. 6151 + 1932
8. 2357 + 821
9. 3663 + 249
10. 4545 + 2277
11. 1234 + 888
12. 4355 + 3769

D

Find the missing digits.

1.
```
  ?431
+ 42?1
─────
 5682
```

2.
```
  5?14
+  39?
─────
 5605
```

3.
```
  ?136
+ 1?27
─────
 23?3
```

4.
```
   422
+ ?22?
─────
 4?44
```

5.
```
  79??
+ ??13
─────
 9569
```

6.
```
  ???6
+  538
─────
 300?
```

7.
```
  61?9
+ 3?41
─────
 915?
```

8.
```
  1?3?
+ ?9?8
─────
 6?12
```

Learning Objectives
To consolidate a written method for adding numbers, involving numbers greater than 1000
To develop estimation skills for calculating approximate answers

E

In each question, two of the sums have the same answer and one is different. Find the answers and write down which is the "odd one out".

1.	(a)	2113 + 536 + 6187	(b)	1108 + 3155 + 4593	(c)	3548 + 2644 + 2644
2.	(a)	732 + 823 + 955	(b)	648 + 1211 + 751	(c)	2031 + 155 + 424
3.	(a)	3131 + 89 + 3220	(b)	2342 + 2345 + 1753	(c)	5166 + 107 + 1157
4.	(a)	2468 + 4682 + 824	(b)	246 + 6824 + 904	(c)	2846 + 2648 + 2482
5.	(a)	1111 + 1111 + 1111	(b)	888 + 1555 + 888	(c)	1335 + 999 + 999
6.	(a)	6165 + 1561 + 1651	(b)	5116 + 1156 + 3105	(c)	3156 + 5561 + 560
7.	(a)	1353 + 2464 + 3575	(b)	131 + 242 + 7519	(c)	5313 + 1535 + 544
8.	(a)	4664 + 2242 + 2004	(b)	6226 + 2622 + 42	(c)	4224 + 2224 + 2442

Think for yourself ...

"Interesting" Numbers (I)

With four-digit numbers, it is possible to make some interesting patterns with the digits – for example 1234, 2468, 8765.

(a) Write down as many numbers with "interesting" digit patterns as you can.
(b) Pick two of your numbers and add them together. Do you get an "interesting" answer or not? (Hint – you can use the same number twice if you like.)
(c) Try other pairs of "interesting" numbers. Which ones give "interesting" answers? Is there a rule for this?
(d) Try it with three "interesting" numbers, or more.
(e) Can you make "interesting" answers from "boring" numbers?

Addition 8

Mental strategies

Keywords ● sum ● total ● add ● round up ● round down

A

Add 9 to these numbers.
Write the first six like this: $23 + 9 = 23 + 10 - 1 = 33 - 1 = 32$

1. 34   **3.** 92   **5.** 981
2. 76   **4.** 365   **6.** 4562

Now do these in your head.

7. 83 + 9   **9.** 565 + 9   **11.** 2553 + 9
8. 24 + 9   **10.** 397 + 9   **12.** 43 305 + 9

B

Add 99 to these numbers.
Write the first six like this: $267 + 99 = 267 + 100 - 1 = 367 - 1 = 366$.

1. 325   **3.** 76   **5.** 6375
2. 631   **4.** 954   **6.** 7933

Now do these in your head.

7. 234 + 99   **9.** 923 + 99   **11.** 5941 + 99
8. 687 + 99   **10.** 1667 + 99   **12.** 32 079 + 99

C

Add 90 to these numbers.
Write the first five like this: $547 + 90 = 547 + 100 - 10 = 647 - 10 = 637$.

1. 340   **3.** 45   **5.** 4922
2. 633   **4.** 8780

Now do these in your head.

6. 875 + 90   **8.** 37 + 90   **10.** 9933 + 90
7. 428 + 90   **9.** 1765 + 90

Learning Objectives
To be able to use a rounding and adjustment strategy for adding numbers
To use this strategy when adding other numbers

D

Each function machine has five numbers that are fed into it. Copy the table. Before you do each question, write down the **rule** you will use to work out the output numbers (for example, "add 39" would become "add 40 and subtract 1"). Then work out the output numbers and fill in the last column.

	Input numbers	Machine	Output numbers
1.	45, 26, 87, 145, 561	+ 29	
2.	234, 45, 775, 1256, 6666	+ 79	
3.	522, 956, 2008, 72, 7476	+ 49	
4.	89, 377, 1024, 2116, 65 665	+ 89	
5.	533, 25, 5325, 78 348, 90 0023	+ 19	
6.	2555, 44 83 443, 360, 9392, 56 388	+ 69	

E

The instructions for this section are the same as for section **D**.

	Input numbers	Machine	Output numbers
1.	3345, 426, 867, 4145, 9561	+ 999	
2.	23, 6234, 425, 7875, 1256	+ 990	
3.	1522, 9560, 208, 782, 22 746	+ 900	
4.	455, 89, 1024, 77 216, 65	+ 199	
5.	522, 6363, 7004, 23 123, 90	+ 699	
6.	355, 6272, 8005, 453, 672 311	+ 499	

Think for yourself...

More rules, OK? (I)

In the sections above you have learned to use shortcuts to speed up your mental addition.

(a) Write down, in words, the mental shortcuts for "add 9999", "add 99 999" and "add 999 999".
(b) Can you write rules for "add 9000", "add 90 000", "add 900 000", "add 9900", "add 99 000" and "add 990 000"?
(c) What about other combinations of 9s and zeroes?
(d) What about "add 95", "add 950", "add 995"? Can you think of any more?

Addition 9

Mixed addition problems

Keywords • sum • total • add

A

Carry out these additions. Some will need to be set out in columns, others you will be able to answer by using a mental method.

1. 101 + 2054
2. 6665 + 434
3. 56 362 + 24 113
4. 76 336 + 1000
5. 234 + 567

6. 744 532 + 262 180
7. 342 112 + 3554
8. 1 500 000 + 75 000
9. 1 + 11 + 111 + 1111 + 11 111
10. 352 + 78 943 + 5400

B

Can you find your way through the addition maze? You need to get from 0 to 1000 using only the *correct* answers in the grey squares.

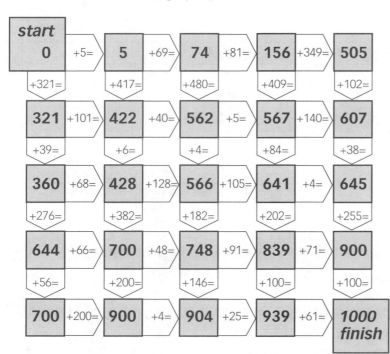

Learning Objectives
To be able to select a mental or written method for adding different numbers
To consolidate a written method for adding numbers

C

Copy and complete these "magic triangles". The total along all three sides of each one must be the same.

1.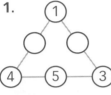

3.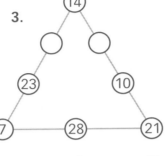

5.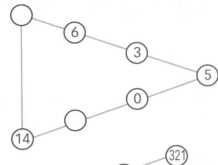

2.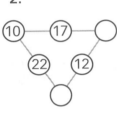

4.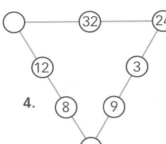

6.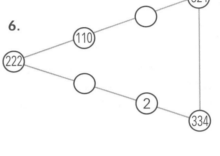

D

Copy and complete these magic squares. Remember – the total along each row, column and diagonal must be the same.

1.

4	2	9
1		6

2.

		10
	6	
2		7

3.

24		
	27	
22		30

4.

	110	
	100	
135	90	

5.

1750		
2468	1543	2772

Think for yourself ...

One-to-nine Sums

(a) Using all the digits from 1 to 9 in order, how many different sums can you make? (Examples: 123 + 456 + 789 = 1368; 1234 + 567 + 89 = 1890.)

(b) What are the smallest and largest answers? Are any of the answers the same?

(c) Try the same thing with the digits in reverse order (9, 8, ... 1). Do any of the answers from part (a) match?

(d) What happens if you are allowed to use 0? Would you put it at the start or the end?

Adding several numbers

Keywords • sum • total • add • column • carry • list

A

1. Find the total area of the Earth's major oceans (all figures in square km):
   Pacific – 165 384 000, Atlantic – 82 217 000, Indian – 73 481 000, Arctic – 14 056 000.

2. Do the same with the major deserts:
   Sahara – 9 065 000, Australian – 1 550 000, Arabian – 1 300 000, Gobi – 1 295 000,
   Kalahari – 520 000.

3. Find the total land area of the Earth's largest islands:
   Greenland – 2 175 600, New Guinea – 808 510, Borneo – 751 900, Madagascar – 594 180,
   Sumatra – 524 100, Baffin Island – 476 070, Honshu – 230 455, Great Britain – 229 880,
   Ellesmere – 212 690, Victoria Island – 212 200.

B

Here are the by-election results in four voting areas ("constituencies").

Party	Constituency				Total
	Horndean	Watcham	Ashfen South	Mallington	
Conservative	10 875	9421	4305	15 224	
Labour	21 385	11 670	3042	17 533	
Liberal Democrat	5241	10 544	2266	18 640	
Green	235	157	54	488	
Independent	100	1456	46	–	
Total					

Copy and complete the table by working out:
(a) the total number of votes cast in each constituency;
(b) the total number of votes gained by each party across the four constituencies.
(c) Check that when you total the results from (a) you get the same as the total of the
   results from (b).

C

For this activity, you need a copy of the data sheet **1995 World Athletics Championships**.

1. Find the total points scored by these teams in the heats: Germany (GER), USA (USA) and Russia (RUS).
2. Find the total points scored by countries that were part of the former Soviet Union: Russia (RUS), Lithuania (LIT) and Belarus (BLR).
3. Which heat produced the greatest points total overall? Why?

Think for yourself...

Speculate!

The Internet is growing very fast and has more and more users each year. This list tells you how many people got "wired" since the Internet was created.

Up to 1986 – 2000, in 1987 – 3000, 1988 – 23 000, 1989 – 33 000, 1990 – 103 000, 1991 – 154 000, 1992 – 304 000, 1993 – 696 000, 1994 –904 000, 1995 – 2 635 000, 1996 – 4 620 000, 1997 – 8 166 000.

Work out how many Internet users there were at the end of 1997.

Using this information, is it possible to predict how many users there will be in 1998, 1999, 2000, ... ? You could find out what the actual figures are and test your prediction.

Subtraction 1

Subtraction bonds to 20

Keywords • take away • subtract • subtraction • leave • left • minus • difference • less than

A

Here are some groups of three numbers. Put signs in between the numbers so that they make a correct sum. You can have one "−" and one "=". You can use the numbers in any order. Warning! One of them is a trick question – can you find it?

1.	4	3	1	**5.**	2	7	9	**9.**	2	4	2
2.	1	8	7	**6.**	3	7	4	**10.**	9	3	6
3.	6	5	1	**7.**	10	7	3	**11.**	2	3	5
4.	4	5	8	**8.**	2	8	6	**12.**	5	5	10

B

Here is a subtraction question: 10 − 9 = 1.
Write down all the other ones you can think of that start with 10. How can you be sure you've found them all?

C

Copy and complete these subtractions.

1.	2 − 1 =	**5.**	4 − 3 =	**9.**	8 − 2 =
2.	3 − 1 =	**6.**	7 − 3 =	**10.**	6 − 3 =
3.	5 − 2 =	**7.**	5 − 1 =	**11.**	6 − 2 =
4.	9 − 4 =	**8.**	9 − 6 =	**12.**	8 − 5 =

D

Here is a subtraction question: 20 − 5 = 15.
Write down all the other ones you can think of that start with 20. How can you be sure you've found them all?

Learning Objectives
To know the subtraction facts to 20
To use the inverse relationship between addition and subtraction to learn these facts

E

Work out what each question means, then write out the sum and work out the answer. When you have found the answer, write it in **words**.

1. Find the difference between six and fourteen.
2. What is left when five is taken from twelve?
3. How much is four less than eleven?
4. Subtract eight from thirteen.
5. What is sixteen minus four?
6. Work out ten minus five.
7. What is left when fifteen is taken from fifteen?
8. How much is eleven less than sixteen?
9. What is the difference between twelve and nine?
10. Subtract two from twelve.

F

Each function machine has five numbers that are fed into it. Copy the table, then work out the output numbers and fill in the last column.

	Input numbers	Machine	Output numbers
1.	5, 6, 7, 8, 9	– 3	
2.	6, 7, 8, 9, 10	– 5	
3.	12, 14, 16, 18, 20	– 9	
4.	11, 13, 15, 17, 19	– 7	
5.	15, 12, 9, 6, 3	– 2	
6.	20, 19, 17, 14, 10	– 6	

Think for yourself ...

Patterns

In the input and output numbers from the machines in section F, there are lots of patterns.

(a) Look carefully at the numbers and write down any patterns you find.
(b) Carry on each pattern with five more numbers. They must use the same rules. If you reach 0 before you have written five, stop. Do you notice anything about the patterns in the input and output for each machine?
(c) Now make up some of your own. You need a set of input numbers with a rule, and a subtraction machine like the ones in section F.
(d) You could make some of your results from (c) into questions for your neighbour. They have to work out the output numbers and write down what the patterns are.

Missing numbers

Keywords ● take away ● subtract ● subtraction ● leave ● left ● minus ● difference
● less than ● inverse

A

Each of these has a number missing. Copy and complete the sum.

1. 12 – ? = 9
2. 14 – ? = 6
3. 10 – ? = 5
4. 9 – ? = 7

5. 16 – ? = 10
6. ? – 4 = 10
7. ? – 11 = 7
8. ? – 7 = 3

9. ? – 9 = 8
10. ? – 4 = 9
11. 8 – 8 = ?
12. 13 – ? = 13

B

Work out the answers to these.

1. 12 – 3 – 4
2. 14 – 5 – 6
3. 15 – 11 –1
4. 16 – 3 – 3

5. 8 – 2 – 5
6. 14 – 4 – 4
7. 9 – 2 – 3
8. 15 – 6 – 7

9. 14 – 1 – 12
10. 15 – 12 – 1
11. 16 – 2 – 10
12. 19 – 1 – 14

C

Each pair of function machines has five numbers that are fed in. Copy the table, then work out the missing numbers and fill in the blank columns.

	Input numbers	1st Machine	Middle numbers	2nd Machine	Output numbers
1.	1, 2, 3, 4, 5	+ 4		– 3	
2.	5, 6, 7, 8, 9	+ 9		– 1	
3.	10, 12, 14, 16, 18	– 5		+ 2	
4.	7, 10, 13, 16, 19	– 2		– 4	
5.	16, 15, 14, 13, 12	– 8		+ 5	
6.	20, 19, 17, 14, 10	– 2		– 7	

D

Each of these has a number missing. Copy and complete the sum.

1. 12 – 6 – ? = 1   **5.** ? – 1 – 6 = 9   **9.** 12 – ? – 2 = 7
2. 13 – 7 – ? = 5   **6.** ? – 5 – 12 = 3   **10.** 18 – ? – 4 = 7
3. 18 – 6 – ? = 9   **7.** ? – 6 – 7 = 6   **11.** 13 – ? – 6 = 2
4. 15 – 8 – ? = 4   **8.** ? – 2 – 4 = 1   **12.** 15 – ? – 5 = 5

E

Each of these has **two** numbers missing. Find *at least* three different ways of completing each one.

1. 15 – ? – ? = 5   **3.** ? – ? – 3 = 8   **5.** ? – 1 – ? = 9
2. 17 – ? – ? = 5   **4.** ? – 6 – ? = 1

Think for yourself...

Pentagony

This function pentagon has two "branches", starting from the top number.

The function machines on each side are **inverses** of each other (they contain the same numbers, but one is added and the other is subtracted). The answers are compared at the bottom, and **NO** is written inside if they don't match.

Try the same machines with a couple of different starting numbers. Do you get a **YES** with any of your choices? Is there a pattern linking the answers?

Try experimenting with the numbers in the machines (keep the top number fixed to start with). Do any combinations produce a **YES**?

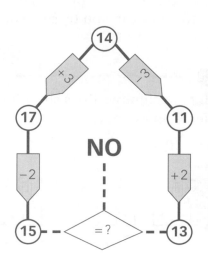

Subtraction 3

Subtracting with tens

> ***Keywords*** ● take away ● subtract ● subtraction ● leave ● left ● minus ● difference ● less than

A

Here are some groups of three numbers. Put signs in between the numbers so that they make a correct sum. You can have one "−" and one "=". You can use the numbers in any order. Warning! One of them is a trick question – can you find it?

1.	90 20 70	**5.**	40 70 30	**9.**	20 40 60
2.	40 20 20	**6.**	20 30 30	**10.**	10 70 80
3.	60 50 10	**7.**	30 40 70	**11.**	50 90 40
4.	80 90 10	**8.**	40 60 20	**12.**	60 80 20

B

Here is a subtraction question: 100 − 90 = 10.
Write down all the other ones you can think of that start with 100 and finish with a multiple of 10. How can you be sure you've found them all?

C

Use the **Number lines** sheet for this section. Show the answers with an arrow.
Here's an example:

36 − 10 = ?

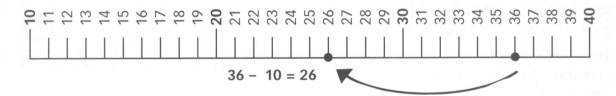

36 − 10 = 26

1.	42 − 10 = ?	**6.**	54 − 20 = ?
2.	73 − 10 = ?	**7.**	68 − 10 = ?
3.	15 − 10 = ?	**8.**	81 − 20 = ?
4.	42 − 20 = ?	**9.**	37 − 10 = ?
5.	27 − 20 = ?	**10.**	33 − 20 = ?

Learning Objectives
To use known subtraction facts to calculate the subtraction of multiples of ten
To be able to subtract any multiple of ten from a TU number

D

Find the missing number that makes each line true.

1.	51 – ? = 41	**5.**	85 – ? = 45	**9.**	? – 50 = 22
2.	61 – ? = 41	**6.**	89 – ? = 39	**10.**	? – 20 = 69
3.	57 – ? = 37	**7.**	88 – ? = 78	**11.**	? – 40 = 51
4.	77 – ? = 47	**8.**	? – 60 = 13	**12.**	95 – ? = 15

E

Each function machine has five numbers that are fed into it. Copy the table, then work out the output numbers and fill in the last column.

	Input numbers	Machine	Output numbers
1.	23, 24, 25, 26, 27	– 10	
2.	56, 57, 58, 59, 60	– 20	
3.	72, 74, 76, 78, 80	– 50	
4.	81, 85, 89, 103, 107	– 70	
5.	40, 50, 60, 70, 80	– 30	
6.	60, 50, 40, 30, 20	– 10	

Think for yourself...

Two-way Ten-splits

Pick any number between 10 and 100.

Write down all the subtractions you can find that have your number as the answer, using two-digit numbers, and that involve multiples of 10 (for example, 74 could be written as 84 – **10**, 94 – **20**, **80** – 6 and **90** – 16).

Try this out with different numbers. Which one has the most subtractions? Which one has the least? Why?

Is there a rule that lets you know how many subtractions a number will have, without trying to write them all down?

Subtraction 4

Tens and units

A

For each of these, write a sum in figures, then write the answer in words.

1. ten minus six
2. eight taken from ten
3. eight less than thirty
4. forty subtract three
5. seventy take away one
6. nine less than twenty
7. take six off fifty
8. eight taken from eighty
9. the difference between ninety and two
10. forty minus four
11. sixty take away seven
12. Write one like this that will give an answer equal to the day of the month you were born (e.g. if you were born on August 22nd, you could use "thirty minus eight" to make 22).

B

Find the missing numbers.

1. $40 - ? = 34$
2. $? - 40 = 1$
3. $30 - ? = 29$
4. $60 - ? = 55$
5. $? - 20 = 3$
6. $90 - ? = 89$
7. $? - 4 = 46$
8. $80 - ? = 77$
9. $? - 2 = 58$
10. $? - 7 = 23$
11. $70 - ? = 64$
12. $? - 8 = 62$

C

Work out the answers to these.

1. $23 - 2$
2. $19 - 7$
3. $53 - 1$
4. $38 - 5$
5. $79 - 3$
6. $88 - 1$
7. $68 - 5$
8. $99 - 6$
9. $44 - 4$
10. $37 - 2$

D

Each function machine has five numbers that are fed into it. Copy the table, then work out the output numbers and fill in the last column.

	Input numbers	Machine	Output numbers
1.	13, 14, 15, 16, 17	– 2	
2.	22, 24, 26, 28, 30	– 4	
3.	46, 47, 48, 49, 50	– 5	
4.	50, 54, 58, 62, 66	– 9	
5.	93, 88, 83, 78, 73	– 6	
6.	35, 30, 26, 23, 21	– 7	

E

Find the missing numbers.

1. $45 - ? = 39$
2. $? - 5 = 51$
3. $32 - ? = 30$

4. $67 - ? = 65$
5. $? - 5 = 23$
6. $82 - ? = 77$

7. $? - 6 = 52$
8. $90 - ? = 81$
9. $? - 8 = 37$

10. $? - 7 = 20$
11. $84 - ? = 79$
12. $? - 4 = 67$

Think for yourself ...

Chopped!

Take any two-digit number (say, 23) and "chop" it – use the two digits as separate numbers (2 and 3) and subtract these from the original number:

$23 - 2 - 3 = 18$.

So 23 "chopped" is 18, and 61 "chopped" is $61 - 6 - 1 = 54$.

(a) Try finding out what happens when you chop various numbers.
(b) What can you say about the results? Is there a rule to help you predict the result of a chop without having to work it out? Are there any numbers that *can't* be the result of a chop?
(c) What happens if you make a "chop chain" – chop a number, then chop the result, chop that one, and so on?
(d) What happens if you use larger numbers?

Subtracting two-digit numbers

Keywords ● take away ● subtract ● subtraction ● leave ● left ● minus ● difference ● less than

A

Each pair of function machines has three numbers that are fed in. Copy the table, then work out the missing numbers and fill in the blank columns. Be careful with part 6!

	Input numbers	1st Machine	Middle numbers	2nd Machine	Output numbers
1.	63, 64, 65	− 20		− 3	
2.	59, 58, 57	− 30		− 7	
3.	74, 73, 72	− 50		− 1	
4.	83, 86, 89	− 40		− 2	
5.	99, 89, 79	− 70		− 6	
6.	19, 17, 15	+ 30		− 5	

Now, for each part, draw a **single** function machine that will do the same job as the two machines together.

B

Do these **in your head**. You can split the work up into two steps.
Example: 57 − 13 = 57 − 10 − 3 = 47 − 3 = 44.

1. 25 − 13
2. 45 − 22
3. 67 − 31
4. 76 − 53

5. 84 − 12
6. 66 − 21
7. 54 − 24
8. 75 − 14

9. 88 − 41
10. 45 − 43
11. 75 − 22
12. 46 − 33

C

Find the missing numbers.

1. 57 − ? = 34
2. ? − 43 = 54
3. 59 − ? = 23
4. 78 − ? = 56

5. ? − 15 = 42
6. 89 − ? = 35
7. ? − 67 = 32
8. 77 − ? = 41

9. ? − 18 = 51
10. ? − 46 = 23
11. 94 − ? = 41
12. ? − 25 = 64

D

This diagram shows a pair of numbers whose difference is 32.

53 → 32 ← 21

1. Draw four more diagrams like this one to show pairs of numbers whose difference is 32.

For each of these questions, draw five diagrams like the ones above.

2.

3.

4.

5. → 46 ←

E

Use any method you can to answer these.

1. 52 – 38
2. 54 – 26
3. 48 – 27

4. 86 – 46
5. 73 – 19
6. 48 – 34

7. 65 – 17
8. 63 – 28
9. 41 – 29

10. 53 – 28
11. 93 – 56 – 24
12. 47 – 27 – 17

F

What's different about these? Answer them to find out.

1. ? – 55 = 51
2. ? – 94 = 24

3. ? – 56 = 62
4. ? – 25 = 88

5. ? – 77 = 59
6. ? – 85 = 58

Think for yourself ...

Flipdiffs

Pick any two-digit number (suppose you pick 23). Reverse the digits (you now have 32). Find the difference between the reversed number and the original (32 – 23 = 9). So 23 has a "flipdiff" of 9. Find other numbers that have a flipdiff of 9. What do they have in common? How many are there? How can you be sure you've found them all?

Try a different starting number. Find the other numbers that give the same flipdiff as this one. Are there more or less of these than the "9"s? Why do you think that is? Can you find a rule that will let you predict a number's flipdiff without having to work it out?

Start with any number and make a "flipdiff chain" – in other words, find its flipdiff, then the flipdiff of that, etc. What happens eventually?

Subtraction 6

Subtraction and addition

Keywords • subtract • difference • add • opposite • inverse • undo

A

Example: $65 - 22 = 43$ because $43 + 22 = 65$.
Write sentences like this for each question.

1.	$35 - 13 = ...$	**5.**	$94 - 17 = ...$	**9.**	$108 - 41 = ...$
2.	$46 - 21 = ...$	**6.**	$66 - 38 = ...$	**10.**	$125 - 43 = ...$
3.	$52 - 31 = ...$	**7.**	$44 - 27 = ...$	**11.**	$132 - 28 = ...$
4.	$76 - 53 = ...$	**8.**	$75 - 69 = ...$	**12.**	$114 - 39 = ...$

B

Example: $61 - 36 = ? - 18$.
Answer: $61 - 36 = 25$ and $25 + 18 = 43$, so $? = 43$.

1.	$34 - 12 = ? - 52$	**3.**	$88 - 53 = ? - 24$	**5.**	$46 - 19 = ? - 54$
2.	$75 - 44 = ? - 36$	**4.**	$51 - 37 = ? - 62$	**6.**	$74 - 58 = ? - 25$

Example: does $49 - 18 = 65 - 37$?
You could just work out both sides, but try this:
$49 - 18 = 31$ and $31 + 37 = 68$. $68 \neq 65$, so the answer is **NO**.
(the $\neq$ symbol means "is not equal to".)

7.	Does $46 - 24 = 67 - 45$?	**9.**	Does $72 - 41 = 54 - 33$?	**11.**	Does $61 - 28 = 85 - 42$?
8.	Does $35 - 24 = 53 - 42$?	**10.**	Does $55 - 36 = 28 - 9$?	**12.**	Does $82 - 59 = 46 - 23$?

C

Example: $82 - 31 = 51$. This fact can be used to answer many other, similar questions.
$82 - 32 = 50$, $82 - 33 = 49$, $82 - 34 = 48$, etc. $82 - 30 = 52$, $82 - 29 = 53$, etc.
$82 - 41 = 41$, $82 - 51 = 31$, $82 - 61 = 21$, etc. $82 - 21 = 61$, $82 - 11 = 71$, etc.
For each question, work out the first one, then use patterns to answer the others.

1.	$55 - 23$.	$55 - 24, 55 - 25, 55 - 26$.	$55 - 22, 55 - 21, 55 - 20$.
2.	$78 - 47$.	$78 - 57, 78 - 67, 78 - 77$.	$78 - 37, 78 - 27, 78 - 17$.
3.	$62 - 48$.	$62 - 49, 62 - 50, 62 - 51$.	$62 - 47, 62 - 46, 62 - 45$.
4.	$125 - 78$.	$125 - 88, 125 - 98, 125 - 108$.	$125 - 68, 125 - 58, 125 - 48$.

D

This table shows the stock of balloons left in a party shop at the end of each day.

		Colour				Total
		Red	Yellow	Blue	Gold	
Number in stock at the end of:	Monday	99	108	75	45	327
	Tuesday	76	94	75	44	289
	Wednesday	73	85	70	44	272
	Thursday	61	82	62	40	245
	Friday	52	70	48	35	205
	Saturday	21	35	24	21	101

Work out how many balloons of each colour were sold on Tuesday, Wednesday, etc., and how many balloons in total were sold. You could put your answers into a table like the one above.

E

Work out which two numbers I am thinking of. Warning! One of them is a trick question.

1. Their sum is 25 and their difference is 1.
2. Sum, 36: difference, 12
3. Sum, 45: difference, 17.
4. Sum, 56: difference, 24.
5. Sum, 73: difference, 53.
6. Sum, 72: difference, 50.
7. Sum, 95: difference, 77.
8. Sum, 40: difference, 15.
9. Sum, 61: difference, 29.
10. Sum, 100: difference, 18.

Think for yourself ...

Sums and Differences

(a) Start with any two numbers (say, 5 and 7). Work out their sum (12) and difference (2). Now use these numbers and work out their sum (14) and difference (10). Carry on in this way until you've done this about ten times. You can record your results in a two-column table headed **sum** and **difference**.

(b) Look at your table. Do you notice any patterns in the results? Try to describe them.

(c) Try the same thing using two different starting numbers. Do you get the same patterns?

(d) This time use two-digit numbers as your starters. Do you get the same patterns?

(e) Can you use algebra to describe the patterns? Call the smaller of the two starters a and the larger one b. The first sum will be $b + a$ and the first difference will be $b - a$.

Subtraction 7

Subtracting hundreds

Keywords ● take away ● subtract ● subtraction ● leave ● left ● minus ● difference

A

Do these in your head.

1.	360 – 40	**5.**	760 – 130	**9.**	630 – 360
2.	480 – 60	**6.**	450 – 340	**10.**	940 – 170
3.	530 – 70	**7.**	830 – 620	**11.**	630 – 190
4.	390 – 50	**8.**	540 – 380	**12.**	350 – 260

B

Do these mentally, then check your answers by setting out the sums in columns.

1.	149 – ? = 143	**5.**	256 – ? = 236	**9.**	835 – ? = 535
2.	459 – ? = 451	**6.**	894 – ? = 864	**10.**	862 – ? = 362
3.	357 – ? = 350	**7.**	745 – ? = 725	**11.**	1097 – ? = 597
4.	666 – ? = 656	**8.**	732 – ? = 692	**12.**	1133 – ? = 333

C

Use a "counting-on" method for these (You could use a **Blank number lines** sheet.)

1.	442 – 21	**3.**	185 – 63	**5.**	961 – 26
2.	656 – 32	**4.**	848 – 19	**6.**	557 – 48

D

Work out the answers to these.

1.   747   **3.**   354   **5.**   845
      – 52   – 82   – 75

2.   333   **4.**   763   **6.**   861
      – 91   – 78   – 84

Learning Objectives
To be able to use mental methods and a written method for subtracting numbers greater than 100
To develop estimation skills calculating approximate answers

E

Use a "counting-on" method for these (You could use a **Blank number lines** sheet).

1. 542 – 233
2. 456 – 241
3. 715 – 174
4. 648 – 316
5. 461 – 429
6. 847 – 145
7. 547 – 252
8. 433 – 391

F

Use a written method to answer these.

1. 384 – 382
2. 563 – 358
3. 745 – 175
4. 767 – 484
5. 676 – 511
6. 832 – 584
7. 888 – 777
8. 1065 – 589

Think for yourself …

Five Fives (II)

(a) Using five "5"s, how many different numbers can you make? You can use any number of "5"s (as long as it's not more than 5) and any number of "–" signs.

Here are two examples to start you off: 5 – 5 = 0, 55 – 5 = **50**.

(b) What can you make with four "4"s?
(c) What about six "6"s?
(d) Try some other numbers.
(e) Try mixing up – which makes more numbers, seven "4"s or four "7"s? Which makes the *biggest* number?

Subtraction 8

Mental strategies

Keywords ● add ● subtract ● digit ● column

A

Subtract 9 from these numbers.
Write the first six like this: 23 – 9 = 23 – 10 + 1 = 13 + 1 = 34.

1.	64	**3.**	92	**5.**	891
2.	36	**4.**	425	**6.**	3752

Now do these in your head.

7.	72 – 9	**9.**	556 – 9	**11.**	3773 – 9
8.	26 – 9	**10.**	302 – 9	**12.**	43 305 – 9

B

Subtract 99 from these numbers.
Write the first six like this: 267 – 99 = 267 – 100 + 1 = 167 + 1 = 168.

1.	453	**3.**	135	**5.**	6449
2.	622	**4.**	954	**6.**	7033

Now do these in your head.

7.	533 – 99	**9.**	961 – 99	**11.**	5941 – 99
8.	786 – 99	**10.**	1022 – 99	**12.**	45 096 – 99

C

Subtract 90 from these numbers.
Write the first five like this: 547 – 90 = 547 – 100 + 10 = 447 + 10 = 457.

1.	430	**3.**	182	**5.**	4035
2.	633	**4.**	6782		

Now do these in your head.

6.	772 – 90	**8.**	167 – 90	**10.**	9033 – 90
7.	423 – 90	**9.**	1861 – 90		

Learning Objectives
To be able to use a rounding and adjustment strategy for subtracting numbers
To use this strategy when subtracting other numbers

D

Each function machine has five numbers that are fed into it. Copy the table. Before you do each question, write down the **rule** you will use to work out the output numbers (for example, "subtract 39" would become "subtract 40 and add 1"). Then work out the output numbers and fill in the last column.

	Input numbers	Machine	Output numbers
1.	43, 126, 87, 145, 661	– 39	
2.	234, 145, 785, 2256, 6666	– 69	
3.	584, 921, 2008, 172, 4776	– 29	
4.	169, 447, 1024, 2116, 57 675	– 89	
5.	533, 125, 4425, 40 748, 610 023	– 19	
6.	2335, 4 483 443, 360, 9192, 41 411	– 59	

E

The instructions for this section are the same as for section **D**.

	Input numbers	Machine	Output numbers
1.	3565, 1426, 1867, 4235, 9577	– 999	
2.	1023, 6004, 2426, 7820, 1256	– 990	
3.	1522, 9560, 1208, 3782, 20 746	– 900	
4.	455, 589, 1608, 77 216, 665	– 199	
5.	1522, 6363, 7004, 23 123, 9000	– 799	
6.	355, 6992, 8010, 453, 611 021	– 299	

Think for yourself…

More Rules, OK? (II)

In the sections above you have learned to use shortcuts to speed up your mental subtraction.

(a) Write down, in words, the mental shortcuts for "subtract 9999", "subtract 99 999" and "subtract 999 999".

(b) Can you write rules for "subtract 9000", "subtract 90 000", "subtract 900 000", "subtract 9900", "subtract 99 000" and "subtract 990 000"?

(c) What about other combinations of 9s and zeroes?

(d) What about "subtract 95", "subtract 950", "subtract 995"? Can you think of any more?

Subtraction 9

Subtracting large numbers

Keywords ● thousand ● digit ● column

A

Work these out in your head.

1. 4361 – 2000
2. 5724 – 60
3. 1332 – 800
4. 6367 – 40
5. 7299 – 600
6. 7881 – 2000
7. 5135 – 80
8. 8358 – 900
9. 1623 – 400
10. 6666 – 60

B

You should be able to work these out in your head, but if not, use a "counting–on" method (you could use a **Blank number lines** sheet).

1. 4136 – 1200
2. 5466 – 23
3. 2145 – 430
4. 1376 – 1100
5. 3453 – 180
6. 9046 – 66
7. 2333– 810
8. 4556 – 390
9. 6153 – 58
10. 5861 – 4000

C

Use a "counting-on" method to answer these (you could use a **Blank number lines** sheet).

1. 4215 – 1321
2. 5006 – 833
3. 7404 – 3127
4. 5116 – 522
5. 9164 – 842
6. 4590 – 2373

D

These need to be set out in columns.

1. 3451 – 1932
2. 2350 – 621
3. 2963 – 429
4. 4567 – 2277
5. 1234 – 888
6. 4421 – 2994

Learning Objectives
To consolidate a written method for subtracting numbers, involving numbers greater than 1000
To develop estimation skills for calculating approximate answers

E

Find the missing digits.

1.
```
   414?
 - ?110
 ------
   1036
```

3.
```
   1??8
 - ?405
 ------
    13?
```

5.
```
   5?35
 - 16??
 ------
   ?448
```

7.
```
   ??90
 - 20??
 ------
   1186
```

2.
```
   ?8?9
 - 5166
 ------
    68?
```

4.
```
   303?
 - ?035
 ------
    ??6
```

6.
```
   ?38?
 - 2??9
 ------
   2008
```

8.
```
   ????
 - 7777
 ------
   1296
```

F

In each question, two of the sums have the same answer and one is different. Find the answers and write down which is the "odd one out".

	(a)	(b)	(c)
1.	6116 – 3124 – 1215	8456 – 956 – 5733	2667 – 600 – 290
2.	5000 – 2525 – 2323	456 – 211 – 103	2115 – 8 – 1955
3.	9000 – 6000 – 3000	3030 – 2020 – 1010	4114 – 2112 – 1112
4.	9 – 5 – 2	250 – 125 – 123	9999 – 8752 – 1045
5.	5050 – 2277 – 2700	441 – 222 – 146	2115 – 8 – 1034
6.	8181 – 5400 – 2700	4030 – 3020 – 729	1551 – 662 – 808
7.	751 – 231 – 21	9630 – 8642 – 889	6420 – 5319 – 1002
8.	103 – 8 – 5	1250 – 129 – 1121	3234 – 2341 – 893

Think for yourself…

"Interesting" Numbers (II)

With four-digit numbers, it is possible to make some interesting patterns with the digits – for example 1234, 2468, 8765.

(a) Write down as many numbers with "interesting" digit patterns as you can.
(b) Pick two of your numbers and find the difference between them. Do you get an "interesting" answer or not? (Hint – you can use the same number twice if you like.)
(c) Try other pairs of "interesting" numbers. Which ones give "interesting" answers? Is there a rule for this? Can some "interesting" answers be made in more than one way?
(d) Try it with three "interesting" numbers, or more.
(e) Can you make "interesting" answers from "boring" numbers?

Subtraction 10

Mixed subtraction problems

Keywords ● subtraction ● take away ● difference ● minus ● less than

A

Work these out in your head.

1. 2545 – 644
2. 19 665 – 1434
3. 53 552 – 37 113
4. 76 336 – 7633
5. 100 234 – 567
6. 516 752 – 262 520
7. 124 112 – 5664 – 90 999
8. 1 500 000 – 75 000
9. 11 111 – 1111 – 111 – 11 – 1
10. 10 550 352 – 78 943 – 5400

B

Can you find your way through the subtraction maze? You need to get from 1000 to 0 using only the *correct* answers in the grey squares.

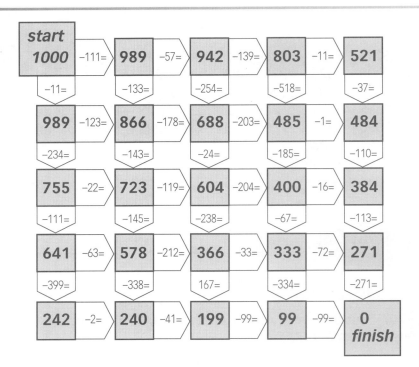

C

This table shows the distances of the planets from the Sun in millions of kilometres.

Name of Planet	Mercury	Venus	Earth	Mars	Jupiter	Saturn	Uranus	Neptune	Pluto
Distance from Sun (million km)	58	108	150	228	779	1426	2870	4493	5898

1. Work out how wide the gaps between the orbits of the planets are.
2. Work out how close each planet can get to the Earth.

Learning Objectives
To be able to select a mental or written method for subtracting different numbers
To consolidate a written method for subtracting numbers

D

This table shows the heights of some mountains in metres.

Name	Country	Volcanic	Height (m)
Everest	Tibet/Nepal	✗	8848
Tengri Khan	Khirghistan	✗	6695
Kilimanjaro	Tanzania	✔	5895
Popocatepetl	Mexico	✔	5453
Mont Blanc	France/Italy	✗	4808
Matterhorn	Switzerland/Italy	✗	4477
Fujiyama	Japan	✔	3776
Parnassus	Greece	✗	2457

1. Work out how much taller each mountain is than the next highest one.
2. Do this with the volcanic mountains only.
3. The highest mountain in the UK is Ben Nevis, at 1344 m. Work out how much taller than Ben Nevis the mountains in the table are.

Think for yourself...

One-to-nine Subtractions

(a) Using all the digits from 1 to 9 in order, how many different subtractions can you make?

(Examples: $123 - 45 - 6 - 7 - 8 - 9 = 48$; $1234 - 567 - 89 = 578$.)

(b) What are the smallest and largest answers? Are any of the answers the same?
(c) Try the same thing with the digits in reverse order (9, 8, ... 1). Do any of the answers from part (a) match?
(d) What happens if you are allowed to use 0? Would you put it at the start or the end?

Multiplication 1

Multiplication

Keywords ● multiply ● times ● product ● grouping ● repeated addition

A

This dot pattern shows the product 3×2.

Draw dot patterns to show these products
(you could use other symbols than dots – stars, squares, etc.).

$3 \times 2 = 6$

1. 4×2	**5.** 2×5
2. 5×2	**6.** 1×4
3. 2×3	**7.** 3×3
4. 3×4	**8.** 5×1

9. 4×4
10. 5×5

B

Write these multiplications as repeated additions.
Example: $2 \times 3 = 3 + 3$.

1. 5×2 **3.** 2×5 **5.** 3×3
2. 5×4 **4.** 4×3 **6.** 2×4

Write these repeated additions as multiplications.
Example: $4 + 4 = 2 \times 4$.

7. $2 + 2$ **9.** $4 + 4 + 4 + 4$ **11.** $4 + 4$
8. $3 + 3 + 3 + 3$ **10.** $3 + 3 + 3 + 3 + 3$ **12.** $1 + 1 + 1 + 1$

C

Find the missing numbers.

1. $2 \times ? = 8$ **4.** $? \times 4 = 12$ **7.** $4 \times ? = 20$ **10.** $? \times 3 = 0$
2. $? \times 3 = 9$ **5.** $? \times 2 = 8$ **8.** $2 \times ? = 2$
3. $5 \times ? = 10$ **6.** $5 \times ? = 15$ **9.** $? \times 1 = 5$

Learning Objectives
To develop the concept of multiplication through grouping and repeated addition
To understand commutativity through the use of arrays

D

Match the additions in the ovals and write statements like this.
Example: 3 + 3 = 2 + 2 + 2 so 2 × 3 = 3 × 2.

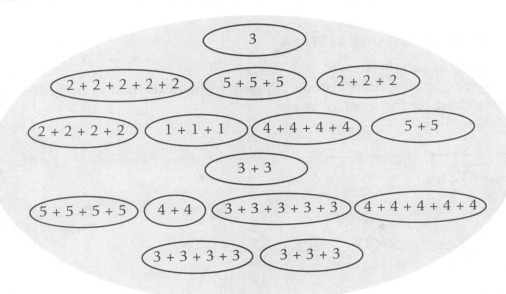

Think for yourself ...

A Multiplication Leaf

You will need a **Multiplication leaf worksheet** for this activity.

(a) Fill in the multiplication square on the worksheet.
(b) Have the numbers checked, then copy them onto the second square.
(c) Now follow the diagonals as marked. Plot a point (dot) on the leaf diagram for each number on the diagonal. Always start at the place marked on the guide line, and only use the positions marked on the guide line. The first three (diagonals 1,2 and 3) have been done for you.
(d) Look for sets of three or more dots arranged in a straight line. If you find any, join them up with a ruler. When you have found all the lines, your picture should be symmetrical, and can be coloured.

Multiplication 2

Know your tables!

Keywords • table • times • multiply • multiple • multiplication

THIS IS A MULTIPLICATION TABLE TEST.

Write down the question and the answer. Your teacher will tell you when to start and how much time you have for each section. You should **clear your desk** apart from this book, whatever you are writing on and a pen or pencil.

A

Both numbers are 5 or less.

1. $2 \times 2 =$	**4.** $3 \times 3 =$	**7.** $4 \times 1 =$	**10.** $5 \times 5 =$
2. $5 \times 3 =$	**5.** $4 \times 2 =$	**8.** $5 \times 2 =$	
3. $3 \times 4 =$	**6.** $2 \times 3 =$	**9.** $4 \times 4 =$	

B

One of the numbers is bigger than 5.

11. $4 \times 7 =$	**14.** $9 \times 4 =$	**17.** $3 \times 7 =$	**20.** $9 \times 5 =$
12. $8 \times 2 =$	**15.** $7 \times 2 =$	**18.** $9 \times 3 =$	
13. $3 \times 6 =$	**16.** $5 \times 6 =$	**19.** $4 \times 10 =$	

C

Both numbers are bigger than 5.

21. $6 \times 6 =$	**24.** $10 \times 7 =$	**27.** $7 \times 6 =$	**30.** $8 \times 9 =$
22. $7 \times 7 =$	**25.** $6 \times 8 =$	**28.** $9 \times 9 =$	
23. $8 \times 8 =$	**26.** $8 \times 7 =$	**29.** $9 \times 6 =$	

Now you will mark the test. Your teacher will read out the answers.

D

Now that your test has been marked, you can analyse which tables you knew well or poorly, or if there were particular questions that caused you problems. To do this, you need a blank multiplication square in your exercise book.

Learning Objectives
To find out the multiplication facts that are not known by individual pupils
To give practice in developing quick recall of these multiplication facts

When this is ready, mark in only the answers that you got **wrong** in the test. For example, if you got 4 × 6 wrong, write the correct answer, **24**, in the "6 × 4" space in the table and in the "4 × 6" space.

If any rows or columns have 3 or more numbers filled in, it is likely that you don't know this table. Write these tables out **in full**, for example:

4 times table

$1 \times 4 = 4$ $2 \times 4 = 8$ $3 \times 4 = 12$, etc.

If any row or column just has one or two numbers filled in, it is likely that these are particular ones that you've forgotten, or never learned in the first place. Write these multiplications out **five times** each.

E

Now sit and say each complete table quietly to yourself, **two or three times**. If your teacher thinks it's a good idea, you could swap books with your neighbour and get him or her to test you on the ones you didn't know. Do the same with the "odd ones" you've written down. Say them to yourself at least **ten times** each. If you also work with your neighbour, he or she could pick questions from this list at random.

F

Your teacher will now **read** you a similar test out loud. The questions will be grouped in the same way, but the numbers will be different. If you have worked carefully this lesson, your score should improve compared to the first test.

Think for yourself ...

Hundred Square Patterns

For this activity, you will need a **Hundred squares sheet**.
(a) Choose a colour. Colour in all the numbers in the 2 × table. There should be a pattern. Carry on until you have coloured every square that fits the pattern.
(b) On a different square, using a different colour, do the same with the 3 × table.
(c) Work through the other tables.
(d) Are any of the patterns similar to each other? Which ones, and why?
(e) What about the tables for numbers bigger than 10? Investigate.

Doubling

Keywords • double • multiply • times

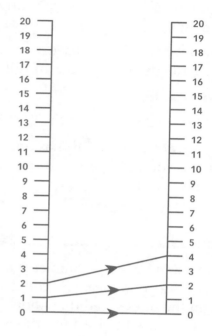

A

To begin this section, write out your 2 × table. You will need to refer to it.

B

Draw two identical vertical scales (number lines) going from 0 to 20, about 5 cm apart (squared paper is best for this). Connect each number on the left-hand scale to its double on the right-hand scale – the first three have been done in the example on the right.

C

Double these numbers.
Write them like this example: Double 24 = 24 × 2 = 48.

1.	10	**5.**	12	**9.**	44	**13.**	41
2.	11	**6.**	24	**10.**	13	**14.**	30
3.	23	**7.**	31	**11.**	14	**15.**	34
4.	32	**8.**	33	**12.**	21		

D

Feed all of these numbers into the doubling machine. Copy the table and fill in the output column.

	Input numbers	Machine	Output numbers
1.	15, 25, 35, 45		
2.	16, 26, 36, 46		
3.	17, 27, 37, 47	**× 2**	
4.	18, 28, 38, 48		
5.	19, 29, 39, 49		

	Input numbers	Machine	Output numbers
6.	50, 60, 70, 80, 90		
7.	51, 61, 71, 81, 91		
8.	53, 63, 73, 83, 93	× 2	
9.	55, 65, 75, 85, 95		
10.	56, 66, 76, 86, 96		
11.	58, 68, 78, 88, 98		
12.	59, 69, 79, 89, 99		

E

1. This grid can be used to show all the numbers from 0 up to 99. Make a copy of this (square dotted paper is best) or use a **Blank 100 grid** sheet.

2. On your grid, join every number to its double (if it's on the grid). The example on the right shows 13 joined to 26, and 45 joined to 90.
   What is the largest number you could start from, and still fit its double on the grid?

3. Start joining numbers to their doubles. Use a sharp pencil and be as careful as you can.

4. Comment on the pattern of lines you have drawn.

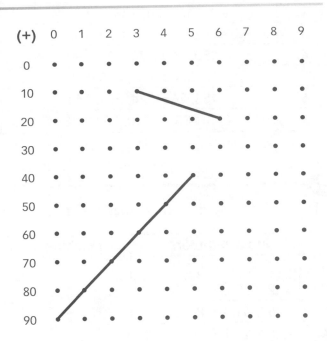

Think for yourself ...

Grid Improvements

There were some numbers on the original grid that couldn't be joined to their doubles.

(a) Solve this problem by designing an improvement to the original grid, and then try out your idea. (Your teacher will help if you're not sure how to do this.)

(b) Does this *really* solve the problem? Why?

(c) There are lots of variations possible on a diagram like this. Try to think of some of them and try them out.

Multiplication 4

Repeated doubling

Keywords ● double ● multiply ● times

A

Feed these numbers into the doubling machine. Copy the table and fill in the output column.

	Input numbers	Machine	Output numbers
1.	101, 103, 105, 107, 109		
2.	116, 126, 136, 146		
3.	217, 227, 237, 247		
4.	150, 160, 170, 180, 190	× 2	
5.	135, 245, 355, 465, 575		
6.	453, 268, 324, 571, 844		
7.	1003, 2034, 1540, 3641, 4884		

B

Use this "double doubling" machine to multiply the input numbers by 4.

	Input numbers	Machine	Middle numbers	Machine	Output numbers
1.	4, 5, 6, 7, 8				
2.	23, 25, 27, 29, 31				
3.	51, 61, 71, 81, 91	× 2		× 2	
4.	120, 130, 140, 150, 160				
5.	113, 223, 333, 443, 553				
6.	653, 248, 304, 570, 634				

Learning Objectives
To be able to double any number mentally and repeat the doubling to multiply by 4 and 8
To use this strategy to multiply by 16, 32 and 64

C

Carry out these multiplications by repeated doubling ($\times$ 8 is doubling 3 times, $\times$ 16 is 4 times, etc.).
You will need some space for working.

	Input numbers	Machine	Output numbers
1.	7, 8, 5, 9	$\times$ **8**	
2.	16, 21, 26, 31		
3.	38, 58, 78, 98		
4.	12, 23, 34, 45	$\times$ **32**	
5.	56, 53, 50, 47		
6.	65, 91, 34, 67		
7.	11, 13, 15, 16, 17	$\times$ **16**	
8.	51, 61, 71, 81, 91		
9.	68, 42, 56, 73, 18		
10.	12, 27, 53, 43, 26	$\times$ **64**	
11.	14, 26, 54, 38, 86	$\times$ **128**	
12.	30, 21, 53, 66, 37	$\times$ **256**	

D

Use repeated doubling to find the missing numbers in these questions.

1. $11 \times ? = 22$
2. $23 \times ? = 92$
3. $53 \times ? = 424$

4. $14 \times ? = 224$
5. $65 \times ? = 260$
6. $20 \times ? = 640$

7. $? \times 75 = 4800$
8. $? \times 81 = 648$
9. $? \times 47 = 6016$

10. $? \times 91 = 364$
11. $? \times 28 = 7168$
12. $? \times 48 = 96$

Think for yourself ...

Make a Million (I)

(a) Start with 2. Double it repeatedly until your answer becomes bigger than a million (has seven digits). Keep a record of how many doublings it takes.

(b) You are going to work up with different starting numbers (3 will be next). Do you need to do 4?

(c) When you have a number of results, use them to produce a graph of "starting number" against number of doublings needed.

Multiples of ten

Keywords ● multiple ● multiply ● times ● product ● place ● column ● zero

A

Feed these numbers into the × 10 machine. Copy the table and fill in the output column.

	Input numbers	Machine	Output numbers
1.	5, 7, 9, 11, 13		
2.	25, 35, 45, 55, 65		
3.	91, 87, 83, 79, 75	× **10**	
4.	102, 104, 106, 108, 110		
5.	236, 347, 458, 569, 680		
6.	1452, 1674, 1896, 2118, 2340		

B

Feed these numbers into the × 100 machine. Copy the table and fill in the output column.

	Input numbers	Machine	Output numbers
1.	14, 12, 10, 8, 6		
2.	53, 43, 33, 23, 13		
3.	171, 167, 163, 159, 155	× **100**	
4.	426, 537, 648, 759, 870		
5.	1553, 1775, 1997, 2219, 2441		

C

Find the missing numbers in these calculations.

1. $6 \times ? = 600$
2. $15 \times ? = 150$
3. $26 \times ? = 260$

4. $? \times 100 = 1300$
5. $? \times 10 = 2350$
6. $? \times 100 = 10\,700$

7. $18 \times ? = 1800$
8. $951 \times ? = 95\,100$
9. $103 \times ? = 1030$

10. $? \times 10 = 6600$
11. $? \times 10 = 4020$
12. $? \times 100 = 35\,000$

D

Feed these numbers into the machines. Copy the table and fill in the output column.

	Input numbers	Machine	Output numbers
1.	5, 7, 9, 11, 13	× **1000**	
2.	55, 45, 35, 25, 15		
3.	92, 84, 86, 78, 70	× **10 000**	
4.	502, 404, 306, 208, 110		
5.	7, 16, 25, 34, 43	× **1 000 000**	
6.	145, 167, 189, 211, 234		

E

Use your knowledge of multiplication tables to answer these.
Example: $2 \times 6 = 12$, so $20 \times 6 = 120$.

1.	30×5	5.	70×3	9.	700×3	13.	800×7
2.	60×2	6.	8×80	10.	600×4	14.	7×500
3.	80×4	7.	4×90	11.	300×6	15.	4×400
4.	50×5	8.	6×50	12.	200×9	16.	8×900

F

Use your knowledge of multiplication tables to answer these.
Example: $4 \times 8 = 32$, so $4000 \times 80 = 320\,000$.

1.	30×60	4.	7000×30	7.	$900\,000 \times 20$	10.	$2\,000\,000 \times 60$
2.	200×40	5.	40×8000	8.	$80\,000 \times 30$	11.	$400\,000 \times 400$
3.	50×80	6.	500×500	9.	900×7000	12.	80×800

Think for yourself…

Powerful Tens

(a) Copy this line: 100 (2 zeroes) = 10 (1 zero) × 10 (1 zero).
(b) Now write a similar line starting with 1000 (3 zeroes).
(c) Now write **two** lines starting with 10 000, and **two** lines starting with 100 000.
(d) Carry on this pattern, each time writing **as many** lines as you can.
(e) Is there a rule which describes what you have found? Test it out using some really *big* numbers.
(f) What happens if you split a number so that there are **three** numbers being multiplied to make it?

Multiplying two digits by one digit

Keywords ● multiple ● multiply ● times ● product ● place ● column ● zero

A

Use this method to do these multiplications.
Example: $23 \times 4 = (20 \times 4) + (3 \times 4) = 80 + 12 = 92$.

1. 21×8
2. 32×4
3. 56×7

4. 51×5
5. 72×3
6. 36×6

7. 42×9
8. 55×3
9. 46×8

10. 74×6
11. 92×5
12. 99×9

B

Use any mental method to do these.

1. $\begin{array}{r} 31 \\ \times\ 4 \\ \hline \end{array}$
2. $\begin{array}{r} 52 \\ \times\ 3 \\ \hline \end{array}$

3. $\begin{array}{r} 46 \\ \times\ 8 \\ \hline \end{array}$
4. $\begin{array}{r} 21 \\ \times\ 5 \\ \hline \end{array}$

5. $\begin{array}{r} 66 \\ \times\ 3 \\ \hline \end{array}$
6. $\begin{array}{r} 37 \\ \times\ 7 \\ \hline \end{array}$

7. $\begin{array}{r} 24 \\ \times\ 9 \\ \hline \end{array}$
8. $\begin{array}{r} 55 \\ \times\ 5 \\ \hline \end{array}$

9. $\begin{array}{r} 48 \\ \times\ 6 \\ \hline \end{array}$
10. $\begin{array}{r} 75 \\ \times\ 6 \\ \hline \end{array}$

11. $\begin{array}{r} 93 \\ \times\ 6 \\ \hline \end{array}$
12. $\begin{array}{r} 99 \\ \times\ 9 \\ \hline \end{array}$

C

Use the method you prefer to find the numbers in the output column.

	Input numbers	Machine	Output numbers
1.	24, 28, 32, 36, 40	× 3	
2.	66, 63, 60, 57, 54	× 5	
3.	27, 38, 49, 60, 71	× 8	
4.	49, 56, 63, 70, 77	× 7	
5.	35, 37, 41, 49, 65	× 6	
6.	98, 97, 95, 92, 88	× 4	
7.	21, 32, 43, 54, 65	× 9	

D

Copy each diagram, then multiply the numbers at the three corners of each triangle to find the number that goes in the middle. The first one has been done for you.

1.

2.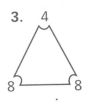

3.

4.

5.

6. 2

E

For each problem, write down and perform the multiplication, using the method you prefer, then write a sentence to give the answer.

1. A crate contains twenty-four egg boxes. Each box contains half-a-dozen eggs. How many eggs will be packed in the crate?
2. A school tuck shop orders thirty-five pints of milk to sell each day. How many do they order in a week?
3. How many corners are there on fifty-five hexagons?
4. Gina's café has forty-nine tables that will seat four people each. If every table is full, how many people are there in the café?
5. On the road where Kohsuke lives, there are thirty-four traffic light poles. Each pole contains three light bulbs. How many light bulbs does his road use?
6. How many limbs do eighty-seven people have?

Think for yourself ...

Any Three Digits

(a) Pick any three digits (example: 1, 2 and 3).
(b) Split them into a two-digit number and a single-digit number to make as many different multiplications as possible. (e.g. 12 × 3, 13 × 2, 32 × 1, etc.) Work out the answers to these multiplications. Are there any connections between the answers?
(c) Change any one of the digits (they don't all have to be different). Work through step (b) with these numbers.
(d) What's similar to last time and what's different?
(e) Change the same digit that you changed in (c) to something new. Repeat steps (b), (c) and (d).
(f) Do this a few more times. Does a pattern emerge?
(g) Try the whole thing over again from a different starting point. Are the results the same?

Multiplication 7

Multiplying larger numbers by one digit

Keywords ● multiple ● multiply ● times ● product ● place ● column ● zero

A

Use this method to do these multiplications.

Example: $2235 \times 6 = (2000 \times 6) + (200 \times 6) + (30 \times 6) + (5 \times 6)$
$= 12\,000 + 1200 + 180 + 30$
$= 13\,410.$

1. 215×7
2. 332×5
3. 586×8

4. 501×9
5. 742×2
6. 326×3

7. 1462×6
8. 2575×5
9. 8426×4

10. 4714×7
11. 6902×8
12. 9999×9

B

Calculate these.

1. $\begin{array}{r} 311 \\ \times\ 6 \\ \hline \end{array}$

2. $\begin{array}{r} 552 \\ \times\ 7 \\ \hline \end{array}$

3. $\begin{array}{r} 406 \\ \times\ 3 \\ \hline \end{array}$

4. $\begin{array}{r} 251 \\ \times\ 4 \\ \hline \end{array}$

5. $\begin{array}{r} 676 \\ \times\ 2 \\ \hline \end{array}$

6. $\begin{array}{r} 357 \\ \times\ 8 \\ \hline \end{array}$

7. $\begin{array}{r} 1294 \\ \times\ 6 \\ \hline \end{array}$

8. $\begin{array}{r} 2575 \\ \times\ 9 \\ \hline \end{array}$

9. $\begin{array}{r} 3438 \\ \times\ 7 \\ \hline \end{array}$

10. $\begin{array}{r} 7005 \\ \times\ 5 \\ \hline \end{array}$

11. $\begin{array}{r} 9136 \\ \times\ 6 \\ \hline \end{array}$

12. $\begin{array}{r} 9999 \\ \times\ 9 \\ \hline \end{array}$

C

Use the method you prefer to find the numbers in the output column.

	Input numbers	Machine	Output numbers
1.	241, 282, 323, 364, 405	× 4	
2.	616, 823, 1030, 1247, 1454	× 5	
3.	627, 538, 2449, 4360, 6271	× 8	
4.	1499, 5567, 635, 703, 3771	× 3	
5.	385, 367, 8441, 6429, 605	× 6	
6.	1098, 3097, 5095, 7092, 9088	× 9	
7.	821, 932, 1043, 1154, 1265	× 7	

D

Copy each diagram, then multiply the numbers at the four corners of each square to find the number that goes in the middle. The first one has been done for you.

1.   2. 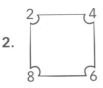   3. 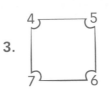   4. 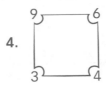   5. 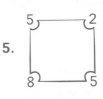   6.

7.   8. 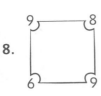   9. 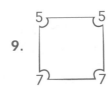   10. 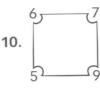   11. 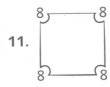   12.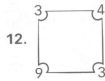

E

For each problem, write down and perform the multiplication, using the method you prefer, then write a sentence to give the answer.

1. How many days are there in three years, if none of them is a leap year?
2. International passenger aircraft fly at about five miles above the ground. There are one thousand, six hundred and nine metres in a mile. How many metres are there in five miles?
3. How many corners are there on eight hundred and eighty-eight squares?
4. Jeff earns eight thousand, four hundred and seventy-five pounds per year. How much money does he earn in six years?
5. A large computer uses eight hard discs with eight hundred and fifty megabytes of storage on each disc. How many megabytes can the computer store altogether?
6. How many tentacles do four hundred and twelve octopuses have?

Think for yourself ...

Make a Million (II)

(a) Copy these lines:

$2 \times 2 = 4$
$2 \times 2 \times 2 = 4 \times 2 = 8$
$2 \times 2 \times 2 \times 2 = 8 \times 2 = 16$

Continue until your answer is a million or bigger. How many 2s do you need?

(b) Copy these lines:

$3 \times 3 = 9$
$3 \times 3 \times 3 = 9 \times 3 = 27$

Carry on until your answer is a million or bigger. How many 3s do you need?

(c) Do the same thing using 4, 5, 6, ... in turn.
(d) Use a graph or bar chart to show your results.

Multiplication 8

Multiplying two digits by two digits

Keywords ● multiply ● product ● place ● column ● zero ● two-digit ● tens ● units ● estimate

A

Work these out in your head.

1.	20×20	**4.**	40×40	**7.**	20×80	**10.**	70×20
2.	40×20	**5.**	80×30	**8.**	30×70	**11.**	60×60
3.	30×30	**6.**	50×90	**9.**	60×70	**12.**	80×90

B

Work these out by multiplying by a single digit, then placing a zero at the end.

1.	21×30	**4.**	33×30	**7.**	35×40	**10.**	85×70
2.	34×20	**5.**	12×80	**8.**	36×50	**11.**	68×90
3.	41×20	**6.**	52×60	**9.**	29×40	**12.**	72×50

C

Use the rectangle method to answer these (here's an example to remind you).

To calculate 23×35:

×	20	3
30	**600**	**90**
5	**100**	**15**

$600 + 100 = 700$
$700 + 90 = 790$
$790 + 15 = 805$

1.	21×16	**3.**	63×41	**5.**	67×55
2.	52×23	**4.**	37×34	**6.**	82×58

D

Set these out in columns to work them out.

1.	99×32	**3.**	81×18	**5.**	37×82
2.	75×45	**4.**	56×65	**6.**	29×61

E

Use the method you like best to work these out.

1.	72×31	**4.**	85×55	**7.**	69×21	**10.**	57×88
2.	35×64	**5.**	75×57	**8.**	78×27	**11.**	53×78
3.	84×26	**6.**	93×25	**9.**	89×62	**12.**	44×44

F

576 can be written as the product of two 2-digit numbers in more than one way:
$576 = 16 \times 36 = 32 \times 18 = 12 \times 48$.
Do the same thing with each of these numbers.

1.	300	**3.**	1275	**5.**	2548
2.	1100	**4.**	630		

Think for yourself ...

Reversing Products

(a) Try investigating this sequence of products:

$11 \times 11 = 121$, $12 \times 21 = 252$, etc., up to 19×91.

(b) Look at the difference between products (what you have to add on to get the next one). What do you notice?

(c) Look at 21×12, 22×22, 23×32 etc. What happens?

(d) What about other "Reversing Products" like this?

(e) Is there a rule that connects them all?

Large numbers

Keywords ● multiply ● product ● place ● column ● zero ● estimate

---

A

Use the rectangle method to answer these (here's an example to remind you).

To calculate 263×35:

×	200	60	3
30	6000	1800	90
5	1000	300	15

$6000 + 1800 + 90 = 7890$
$1000 + 300 + 15 = \underline{1315}$
$\underline{9205}$

1. 215×36
2. 481×23
3. 808×51
4. 448×195
5. 372×372
6. 625×125
7. 2177×81
8. 5061×24
9. 7766×67
10. 1234×123
11. 4096×256
12. 9999×999

B

Work these out by the usual method.

1. 261×13
2. 304×27
3. 419×29
4. 334×344
5. 102×888
6. 525×116
7. 3535×44
8. 3692×17
9. 2999×29
10. 8561×156
11. 6868×912
12. 7202×522

C

To work these out, make a simpler calculation, then add the correct number of zeroes.
Use the rectangle or traditional method.
Example: 6100×520:

$61 \times 52 = 3000 + 50 + 120 + 2 = 3172$.
$6100 \times 520 = 3172\,000$ (adding 3 zeroes).

1. 2120×16
2. 525×430
3. 6310×410
4. $30\,700 \times 304$
5. $6750 \times 55\,500$
6. $825\,000 \times 5830$
7. $1199 \times 3\,200\,000$
8. $757\,500 \times 5400$
9. $811\,800 \times 1\,800\,000$
10. $5\,678\,000 \times 654\,000$
11. $37\,260\,000\,000 \times 8\,210\,000$
12. $2999 \times 611\,000\,000\,000$

D

Use the method you like best to work these out.

1. $22\,314 \times 31$
2. 3534×6421
3. $84\,552 \times 2650$
4. $855\,199 \times 55$
5. $757\,575 \times 575\,757$

6. $93\,000\,000 \times 2561$
7. $69\,365 \times 21\,000\,000$
8. $789\,300 \times 276\,900$
9. $89\,315 \times 6\,241\,550$
10. $576\,879 \times 888\,888$

E

Look for a sensible way of ordering the numbers to make it easier. Use mental methods wherever possible.

1. $300 \times 15 \times 28$
2. $1100 \times 250 \times 128$
3. $1275 \times 4500 \times 363\,600$

4. $631 \times 452 \times 6111 \times 3000$
5. $2548 \times 2548 \times 2548 \times 2548$
6. $1\,000\,000 \times 25\,600 \times 20 \times 2\,048\,000$

Think for yourself ...

Rooting About

(a) You will be looking for an unknown number (call it N) in this section. You will start with a target of 10. This means that you multiply N by itself to get 10 (N is called the **square root** of 10). N is not a whole number, but is found somewhere *between* two whole numbers – your task is to find them. We say that these numbers "cradle" N. This is easy – try some numbers out until you find the answer.

(b) Your next target is 100. This time, the answer is a whole number. Find N.

(c) Try 1000, 10 000, etc. Sometimes the answer is a whole number, sometimes you'll be looking for cradling numbers.

(d) Does a pattern emerge as you go higher?

(e) Extension: investigate the Ns that fit this pattern (hint: the answer is *never* a whole number, so you are always looking for a "cradle").

$N \times N = 10$ (N is the square root of 10);
$N \times N \times N = 100$ (N is the cube root of 100);
$N \times N \times N \times N = 1000$ (N is the fourth root of 1000);
$N \times N \times N \times N \times N = 10\,000$ (N is the fifth root of 10 000); etc.

Multiples

Keywords ● table ● factor ● digit sum ● multiple ● (lowest) common multiple

A

Find all the numbers in each cloud that are multiples of the circled number.

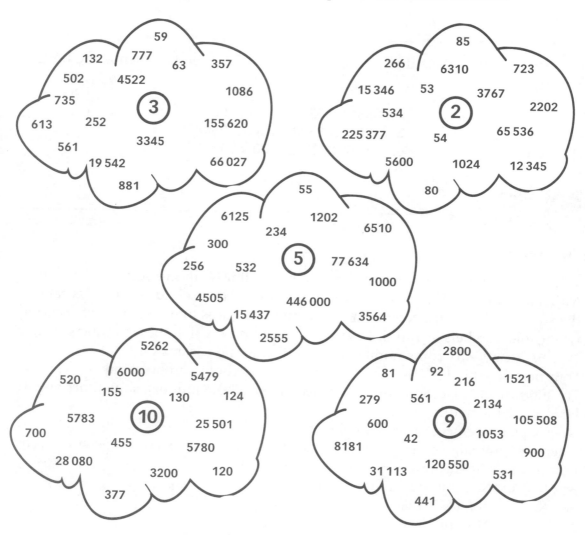

B

Find all the numbers in each box that are multiples of the middle number.

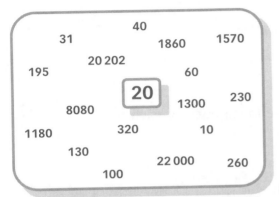

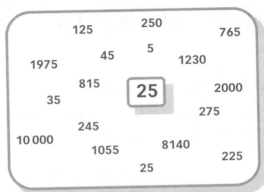

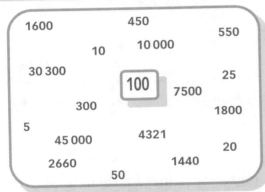

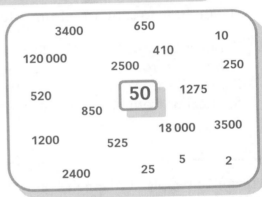

Think for yourself...

Common Multiples

(a) Write down the first 12 multiples of 2, in a column.

(b) Write down the first 12 multiples of 3, in a column next to the first one.

(c) Circle the numbers that occur in **both** columns. These are the common multiples of 2 and 3. They are all multiples of another number. Which one?

(d) If you repeated steps 1 and 2 using multiples of 3 and 5, what number do you think would appear in step 3?

(e) Test it out and see if you were right.

(f) The first number that occurs in both lists is called the **lowest common multiple** of 3 and 5 (or LCM for short). You can easily test for multiples of this number. If the number being tested passes the test for 3 *and* the test for 5, you have a multiple of the LCM.

(g) Devise tests for multiples of 6, 15, 18, 30, 45, 60, 75 and 90 by combining ones you already know. Just write down which tests have to be combined.

Division 1

Division

Keywords ● division ● divide ● share ● split ● group

A

In each question, work out how many times you have to subtract to reach 0.

Example: Subtracting 2s from 8.
$$8 - 2 = 6 \quad (1)$$
$$6 - 2 = 4 \quad (2)$$
$$4 - 2 = 2 \quad (3)$$
$$2 - 2 = 0. \quad (4)$$

Answer: you have to subtract 2 from 8 **four** times.

1.	Subtract 2s from 6.	**5.**	Subtract 4s from 8.	**9.**	Subtract 7s from 21.
2.	Subtract 3s from 6.	**6.**	Subtract 3s from 18.	**10.**	Subtract 6s from 30.
3.	Subtract 2s from 10.	**7.**	Subtract 4s from 16.	**11.**	Subtract 8s from 32.
4.	Subtract 3s from 9.	**8.**	Subtract 5s from 20.	**12.**	Subtract 10s from 50.

B

There are 24 people at Alannah's party. She has organised games for them to play, and needs to split them into teams, with the same number of people on each team so that the games are fair. To help her, she draws a diagram showing 24 people:

The first game is called "Boat Race". She needs 2 teams for this. This is what her diagram looks like when she has divided up the people.

How many people are on each Boat Race team?

Draw diagrams like this, or use **The idea of division** sheet, to work out how many people are on each team for these games, then write a sentence to describe the each answer.

(a) Twister – 4 teams. (b) Charades – 8 teams. (c) Consequences – 3 teams.
(d) Pop Quiz – 6 teams. (e) Three-legged Musical Chairs – 12 teams.

C

Find the things in the cloud that mean the same as each other.

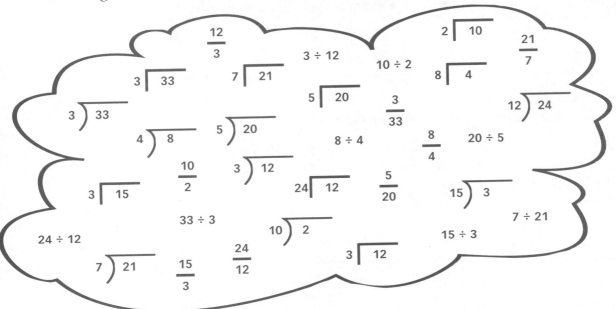

D

Illustrate each division on a diagram, and write down the answer.
This example shows the division $12 \div 4 = 3$:

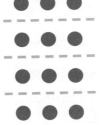

1.	$8 \div 4$	5.	$12 \div 4$	9.	$21 \div 3$
2.	$10 \div 5$	6.	$15 \div 3$	10.	$24 \div 6$
3.	$6 \div 2$	7.	$18 \div 9$	11.	$11 \div 1$
4.	$12 \div 2$	8.	$20 \div 5$	12.	$7 \div 7$

Think for yourself…

Rectangles

(a) For this activity, a set of twelve 1 cm squares would be useful: you could cut some out of squared paper easily. Using these, make six different rectangles. Make a drawing of each rectangle, and mark on it the length and width. Write a division statement like this: 12 ÷ <length> = <width>, putting in your numbers.

(b) Experiment with other numbers of squares – it could be less, or more if you wish. Do any of the arrangements of 1 cm squares form bigger squares?

Division 2

Division and multiplication

Keywords ● divide ● multiply ● share ● multiplication fact ● division fact

---

A

Example: $6 \div 3 = 2$ *because* $2 \times 3 = 6$.
Write similar lines starting with the numbers given.

1. $12 \div 3 = ...$
2. $8 \div 4 = ...$
3. $10 \div 2 = ...$
4. $16 \div 4 = ...$

5. $12 \div 4 = ...$
6. $15 \div 5 = ...$
7. $20 \div 4 = ...$
8. $21 \div 3 = ...$

9. $18 \div 6 = ...$
10. $14 \div 7 = ...$

B

Example: $4 \times 5 = 20$, *so* $20 \div 5 = 4$.
Write similar lines starting with the numbers given.

1. $5 \times 6 = ...$
2. $6 \times 4 = ...$
3. $3 \times 8 = ...$
4. $4 \times 7 = ...$

5. $5 \times 5 = ...$
6. $9 \times 3 = ...$
7. $10 \times 2 = ...$
8. $6 \times 6 = ...$

9. $7 \times 5 = ...$
10. $8 \times 4 = ...$

C

Use the function machines to work out what goes in the Middle and Output columns.

	Input numbers	1st Machine	Middle numbers	2nd Machine	Output numbers
1.	3, 6, 9, 12, 15	÷ 3		× 3	
2.	20, 15, 10, 5, 0	÷ 5		× 5	
3.	4, 12, 20, 28, 36	÷ 4		× 4	
4.	40, 32, 24, 16, 8	÷ 8		× 8	
5.	6, 10, 14, 18, 22	÷ 2		× 2	
6.	0, 6, 12, 24, 48	÷ 6		× 6	

Learning Objectives
To understand the inverse relationship between multiplication and division
To learn the division facts by using the known multiplication facts

D

Copy these and fill in the missing numbers.

1. $14 \div ? = 7$
2. $20 \div ? = 4$
3. $? \div 3 = 7$

4. $? \div 2 = 10$
5. $16 \div 4 = ?$
6. $8 \div ? = 8$

7. $9 \div ? = 3$
8. $? \div 5 = 5$
9. $? \div 7 = 4$

10. $32 \div 8 = ?$
11. $14 \div ? = 2$
12. $? \div 5 = 7$

E

Example:

Copy these diagrams and fill in the missing instructions.

1.   2.   3.   4.   5.

6.   7.   8.   9.   10.

Think for yourself…

Division Statements

(a) Write out the multiplication tables from $1 \times$ to $10 \times$, as division tables (So instead of $2 \times 3 = 6$, you write $6 \div 3 = 2$).

(b) Now write down a set of division statements for each number in turn, using every line you've found for it in (a). Example: $8 \div 8 = 1$,
$$8 \div 4 = 2,$$
$$8 \div 2 = 4,$$
$$8 \div 1 = 8.$$

Division 3

Halving

Keywords • divide • half • halve • halving • quarter

A

Copy and complete these.

1. Half of 2 is …
2. Half of 4 is …
3. Half of 6 is …
4. Half of 8 is …
5. Half of 10 is …
6. Half of 12 is …
7. Half of 14 is …
8. Half of 16 is …
9. Half of 18 is …
10. Half of 20 is …

B

Copy and complete these.

1. Half of 30 is …
2. Half of 40 is …
3. Half of 50 is …
4. Half of 60 is …
5. Half of 70 is …
6. Half of 80 is …
7. Half of 90 is …
8. Half of 100 is …
9. Half of 200 is …
10. Half of 300 is …
11. Half of 400 is …
12. Half of 500 is …
13. Half of 600 is …
14. Half of 700 is …
15. Half of 800 is …
16. Half of 900 is …
17. Half of 1000 is …

C

Use the information about halves of numbers from sections **A** and **B** to answer these.
Example: Half of 48 = half of (40 + 8) = 20 + 4 = **24**.
Find half of …

1. 26   2. 42   3. 84   4. 62   5. 68   6. 36   7. 54   8. 72   9. 58   10. 78

D

Feed these groups of numbers into the "halving machine". Use the method from section C to find the output numbers.

	Input numbers	Machine	Output numbers
1.	116, 126, 136, 146, 156		
2.	404, 408, 412, 416, 420		
3.	922, 940, 958, 966, 974	÷ 2	
4.	7500, 7700, 7900, 8100, 8300		
5.	10 512, 11 524, 12 548, 13 596, 14 692		

Learning Objectives
To be able to halve any even number mentally
To use this strategy to divide by 4

E

Use this "half-and-half-again" machine to find a quarter of the numbers in the input column.

	Input numbers	1st Machine	Middle numbers	2nd Machine	Output numbers
1.	88, 72, 56	÷ 2		÷ 2	
2.	236, 348, 460				
3.	1232, 1364, 1496				

F

Answer these by any method.

1.	266 ÷ 2	**4.**	2264 ÷ 2	**7.**	17 266 ÷ 2	**10.**	105 408 ÷ 2
2.	954 ÷ 2	**5.**	9128 ÷ 4	**8.**	65 292 ÷ 4	**11.**	244 654 ÷ 2
3.	1204 ÷ 4	**6.**	17 264 ÷ 4	**9.**	76 520 ÷ 4	**12.**	1 078 552 ÷ 4

Think for yourself …

Powerful Halving

(a) After what you've seen in sections **E** and **F**, can you think of a way to divide by 8?
(b) What about dividing by 16?
(c) Can you think of any other divisions that you could do in the same way?
(d) Here are some numbers that are guaranteed to "work" by dividing exactly.

Use them to test your ideas.

192, 320, 384, 448, 640, 768, 896, 1280, 1792, 1856, 2624, 3712, 5248, 7424, 8128, 10 496, 16 256, 32 512, 76 864, 153 728, 307 456.

Division 4

Dividing by units

A

In each question, work out how many times you have to subtract to reach 0.

Example: Subtracting 8s from 48.

$$48 - 8 = 40 \quad (1)$$
$$40 - 8 = 32 \quad (2)$$
$$32 - 8 = 24 \quad (3)$$
$$24 - 8 = 16 \quad (4)$$
$$16 - 8 = 8 \quad (5)$$
$$8 - 8 = 0. \quad (6)$$

Answer: you have to subtract 8 from 48 six times.

1. Subtract 4s from 36.
2. Subtract 7s from 42.
3. Subtract 5s from 45.
4. Subtract 9s from 63.
5. Subtract 8s from 64.
6. Subtract 10s from 70.
7. Subtract 6s from 42.
8. Subtract 5s from 75.
9. Subtract 7s from 91.
10. Subtract 4s from 76.
11. Subtract 8s from 96.
12. Subtract 3s from 45.

B

Answer these using a written method.

1. $66 \div 3$
2. $48 \div 4$
3. $94 \div 2$
4. $75 \div 5$
5. $84 \div 7$
6. $96 \div 8$
7. $78 \div 6$
8. $64 \div 4$
9. $81 \div 9$
10. $80 \div 5$
11. $72 \div 3$
12. $84 \div 6$

C

Answer these using a written method.

1. $168 \div 4$
2. $264 \div 6$
3. $535 \div 5$
4. $741 \div 3$
5. $343 \div 7$
6. $652 \div 2$
7. $760 \div 8$
8. $333 \div 9$
9. $544 \div 4$
10. $850 \div 5$
11. $456 \div 8$
12. $852 \div 3$

D

Answer these by dividing a two-digit number by a unit, then adding a zero. If you can use a mental method, do so.

1.	630 ÷ 3	**5.**	720 ÷ 6	**9.**	360 ÷ 9
2.	980 ÷ 7	**6.**	700 ÷ 5	**10.**	560 ÷ 8
3.	560 ÷ 2	**7.**	650 ÷ 5	**11.**	960 ÷ 6
4.	680 ÷ 4	**8.**	690 ÷ 3	**12.**	840 ÷ 7

E

Which answer is "odd one out" (different to the other two)?

1.	(a)	188 ÷ 4	(b)	235 ÷ 5	(c)	432 ÷ 9
2.	(a)	445 ÷ 5	(b)	534 ÷ 6	(c)	855 ÷ 9
3.	(a)	118 ÷ 2	(b)	192 ÷ 3	(c)	128 ÷ 2
4.	(a)	567 ÷ 7	(b)	729 ÷ 9	(c)	240 ÷ 3
5.	(a)	568 ÷ 8	(b)	365 ÷ 5	(c)	497 ÷ 7
6.	(a)	522 ÷ 6	(b)	388 ÷ 4	(c)	261 ÷ 3
7.	(a)	105 ÷ 5	(b)	252 ÷ 9	(c)	168 ÷ 6
8.	(a)	170 ÷ 2	(b)	648 ÷ 8	(c)	255 ÷ 3
9.	(a)	160 ÷ 5	(b)	204 ÷ 6	(c)	224 ÷ 7
10.	(a)	693 ÷ 7	(b)	404 ÷ 4	(c)	495 ÷ 5

Think for yourself ...

Repeated Division

(a) You have seen how repeated halving can help you to divide by other numbers. You can divide repeatedly by other numbers, too, or even combine different ones. Suppose that you didn't like dividing things by 9. How could you do it using 3 instead?

(b) What other numbers could you divide by if you carried on? Use these numbers to test your ideas:
162, 405, 567, 891, 1053.

(c) Can you work out how to divide by 25? Try it with 175, 450, 625, 375, 825.

(d) What about dividing by 15? Try it with 165, 195, 345, 555, 915.

(e) Try out some combinations of your own. Warning – there may be something left over at the end of your calculation: the *remainder*.

Division 5

Remainders

Keywords ● division ● divide ● exact ● left over ● quotient ● remainder

A

Some of these divide exactly, some don't. If a question divides exactly, work out the answer. If it doesn't, find the quotient and **remainder.** You can use the information you know about spotting multiples from *Multiplication 10.*

1. $45 \div 9$
2. $17 \div 2$
3. $33 \div 3$
4. $64 \div 6$

5. $70 \div 5$
6. $31 \div 4$
7. $86 \div 8$
8. $34 \div 7$

9. $25 \div 9$
10. $64 \div 2$
11. $73 \div 5$
12. $30 \div 10$

13. $81 \div 3$
14. $91 \div 5$
15. $48 \div 4$
16. $63 \div 7$

17. $83 \div 2$
18. $56 \div 10$
19. $56 \div 1$
20. $56 \div 8$

B

In this cloud there are lots of divisions.

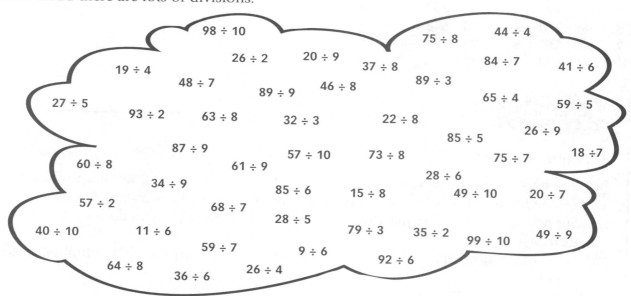

Some divide exactly, some have a remainder of 1, some a remainder of 2, etc. Copy this table, and write each division in the column that matches it. One has been done for you.

Exact	Rem.1	Rem. 2	Rem. 3	Rem. 4	Rem. 5	Rem. 6	Rem. 7	Rem. 8	Rem. 9
$26 \div 2$									

C

For each question, one part has a different remainder to the other two – find out which one.

1.	(a) 273 ÷ 5	(b) 636 ÷ 5	(c) 35 ÷ 2
2.	(a) 343 ÷ 4	(b) 62 ÷ 6	(c) 46 ÷ 4
3.	(a) 254 ÷ 6	(b) 784 ÷ 2	(c) 836 ÷ 3
4.	(a) 785 ÷ 6	(b) 26 ÷ 7	(c) 97 ÷ 5
5.	(a) 637 ÷ 8	(b) 627 ÷ 5	(c) 764 ÷ 6
6.	(a) 868 ÷ 3	(b) 879 ÷ 7	(c) 564 ÷ 5
7.	(a) 536 ÷ 2	(b) 98 ÷ 9	(c) 752 ÷ 8
8.	(a) 768 ÷ 6	(b) 868 ÷ 8	(c) 25 ÷ 7
9.	(a) 365 ÷ 6	(b) 647 ÷ 6	(c) 57 ÷ 6
10.	(a) 560 ÷ 4	(b) 53 ÷ 7	(c) 840 ÷ 5

Think for yourself…

Remainder Spirals

For this activity you need a **Remainder spirals** sheet.

To complete a remainder spiral, follow these instructions.

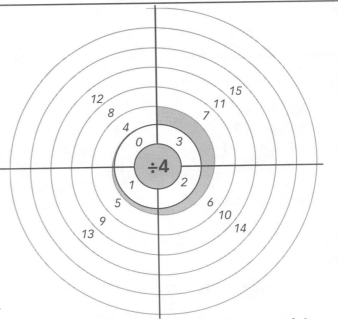

(a) Decide on the number you are going to use to divide. Write it in the centre circle. (÷ 4 has been used as an example).

(b) Divide the spiral into this number of sections (four quarters in the example).

(c) Starting in the top left and going anticlockwise, fill in the white inner ring with the possible remainders (0 for going exactly, 1, 2 and 3 in the example).

(d) Now start putting numbers into the spiral, working anticlockwise (don't write anything in the grey area).

(e) Look at the numbers that end up in each section. What do they have in common? What are the differences between them? Can you invent any rules to describe them?

Dividing larger numbers

Keywords ● division ● divide ● exact ● left over ● quotient ● remainder

A

Carry out these divisions. These divide exactly.

1. $1164 \div 4$
2. $3882 \div 6$
3. $14\,325 \div 3$
4. $47\,260 \div 5$
5. $14\,976 \div 9$
6. $101\,752 \div 7$

These have remainders.

7. $4979 \div 8$
8. $7247 \div 6$
9. $13\,333 \div 3$
10. $56\,467 \div 7$
11. $14\,955 \div 9$
12. $102\,578 \div 4$

B

Find the missing numbers.

1. $1455 \div ? = 5$
2. $1862 \div ? = 7$
3. $23\,484 \div ? = 3$
4. $? \div 6 = 544$
5. $? \div 9155 = 8$
6. $? \div 9 = 24\,884$
7. $680 \div ? = 226 \text{ rem } 2$
8. $7026 \div ? = 7 \text{ rem } 5$
9. $30\,349 \div ? = 6 \text{ rem } 25$
10. $? \div 7 = 158 \text{ rem } 4$
11. $? \div 525 = 4 \text{ rem } 1$
12. $? \div 1666 = 5 \text{ rem } 201$

C

To do these, remove the zeroes from the number, carry out the division, then put the zeroes back.

1. $15\,300 \div 3$
2. $8950 \div 5$
3. $378\,000 \div 9$
4. $14\,700 \div 7$
5. $2\,744\,000 \div 4$
6. $64\,200\,000 \div 6$

These won't work by the method above – divide them the usual way.

7. $24\,350 \div 8$
8. $143\,000 \div 7$
9. $164\,900 \div 4$
10. $13\,000\,000 \div 6$
11. $125\,000 \div 9$
12. $167\,500\,000 \div 3$

D

For each question, write out your working and then give the answer as a sentence.

1. Reg Morris ate 2720 grams of sausages in 3 minutes. What weight of sausages did he consume per minute?

2. The biggest stick of rock ever was made in Blackpool in 1991. It weighed 14 589 oz. An average stick of Blackpool rock weighs about 8 oz. How many ordinary sticks would be equivalent to the giant one?

3. The biggest Cheddar cheese was made in Canada, weighing 78 270 times as much as a normal "supermarket" cheese pack! You normally get about 3 pieces of cheese to a kilogram. How much did the mega-cheese weigh?

4. At the largest wine-tasting ever, 9360 bottles were consumed, with an average of 2 bottles per taster! How many people tasted the wine?

5. The biggest ever pizza was 1472 inches in diameter. How many standard nine-inch pizzas could you make from the same ingredients? (Careful – you have to multiply this number by itself, *then* divide by 9 *twice* to get the answer!)

6. The greatest meat consumption at a barbecue was 31 500 chicken halves in 8 hours. How many halves were eaten each hour?

7. How many whole chickens was that in an hour?

8. The largest ever milk shake would have filled 29 600 cups. How many litres of milk shake were there, assuming that you get 4 cups to the litre?

9. The biggest ever omelette contained 160 000 eggs! How many normal 3-egg omelettes would this many eggs make?

10. In 1995 the Coors Brewery in Colorado brewed 9 374 000 gallons of beer *every week*. How many gallons was that each day, on average?

Think for yourself...

The Real Thing

The most popular soft drink is Coca-Cola, at 573 million drinks consumed every day!

(a) Look at some different time-intervals and try to work out how many Cokes are drunk in them (years, seconds, your lifetime, etc.).

(b) Given that there are approximately six billion people on Earth, how many drinks is that per person per year? How long is it between drinks, on average? Do *you* drink it more or less often than that?

Dividing by two-digit numbers

Keywords ● division ● divide ● exact ● left over ● quotient ● remainder
● estimate ● rough ● approximate ● trial and improvement

A

Some of these divide exactly, some have remainders.

1. 72 ÷ 12
2. 88 ÷ 11
3. 76 ÷ 19

4. 55 ÷ 13
5. 86 ÷ 15
6. 68 ÷ 17

7. 49 ÷ 16
8. 70 ÷ 14
9. 50 ÷ 18

10. 52 ÷ 11
11. 90 ÷ 15
12. 92 ÷ 12

B

Some of these divide exactly, some have remainders.

1. 84 ÷ 21
2. 61 ÷ 30
3. 69 ÷ 23

4. 88 ÷ 35
5. 72 ÷ 36
6. 96 ÷ 32

7. 99 ÷ 24
8. 93 ÷ 55
9. 86 ÷ 43

10. 84 ÷ 28
11. 64 ÷ 63
12. 46 ÷ 64

C

Each pair of divisions either **matches** (the two answers are the same) or **doesn't match** (the two answers are different). Find out which ones match and which don't.

1. (a) 556 ÷ 16 (b) 386 ÷ 11
2. (a) 221 ÷ 13 (b) 275 ÷ 16
3. (a) 630 ÷ 14 (b) 810 ÷ 18
4. (a) 640 ÷ 17 (b) 714 ÷ 19
5. (a) 996 ÷ 12 (b) 925 ÷ 11
6. (a) 728 ÷ 11 (b) 924 ÷ 14
7. (a) 329 ÷ 16 (b) 349 ÷ 17
8. (a) 960 ÷ 15 (b) 969 ÷ 15
9. (a) 607 ÷ 19 (b) 390 ÷ 12
10. (a) 936 ÷ 18 (b) 677 ÷ 13

D

Each machine has five numbers feeding into it. Work out the numbers in the output column.

	Input numbers	Machine	Output numbers
1.	233, 242, 251, 260, 269	÷ 26	
2.	455, 462, 469, 476, 483	÷ 35	
3.	935, 918, 901, 884, 867	÷ 51	
4.	957, 935, 913, 891, 869	÷ 83	
5.	225, 350, 475, 600, 725	÷ 75	
6.	616, 528, 440, 352, 264	÷ 44	

E

Check your answers to section **D** by estimation. Round off the number in the machine to the **nearest ten**, and the output number to the **nearest whole number** (if it has one digit) or the **nearest ten** (if it has two digits), and then multiply these together. You should get something *similar* to the input number, if your answer was correct.

Example: $264 \div 11 = 24$.

Rounded numbers: $10 \times 20 = 200$.

$200 \simeq 264$ (the wiggly $\simeq$ symbol means *is approximately equal to* or *is similar to*).

Think for yourself …

"Hard" Ways and "Easy" Ways

You have seen (in Division 4 *Think for Yourself*) how to divide repeatedly to make division by larger numbers easier. You are going to compare this with the direct method.

(a) Divide 465 by 15:

(i) directly;   (ii) by dividing first by 5 and then by 3.

Which method was easier?   Which method took longer?

(b) Divide 714 by 42:

(i) directly;   (ii) by dividing first by 6 and then by 7.

Which method was easier?   Which method took longer?

(c) Try dividing 854 by 24:

(i) directly;   (ii) by dividing by two suitable single-digit numbers (you have a choice).

What happens?

(d) Try some other comparisons. Ask your neighbour to make up some suitable divisions for you. Tell him or her what number you want to divide by, and that you need one number that divides exactly and one that leaves a remainder. Try to draw some conclusions about which method is "easier" or "harder".

Division 8

Dividing with large numbers

Keywords ● division ● divide ● exact ● left over ● quotient ● remainder ● estimate ● approximate ● trial and improvement

A

Follow these division chains and see where they finish (all of them divide exactly).

1.	750 076 000	÷ 526	**?**	÷ 31	**?**	÷ 125	**?**	÷ 16	**?**					
2.	126 187 740	÷ 18	**?**	÷ 251	**?**	÷ 35	**?**	÷ 7	**?**					
3.	181 794 168	÷ 1031	**?**	÷ 31	**?**	÷ 474	**?**							
4.	396 604 824	÷ 11	**?**	÷ 966	**?**	÷ 28	**?**							
5.	98 733 594 781	÷ 79	**?**	÷ 73	**?**	÷ 71	**?**	÷ 67	**?**	÷ 61				

B

All of these divide exactly.

1. $48\,334 \div 26$
2. $120\,345 \div 113$
3. $630\,729 \div 277$
4. $766\,440 \div 72$
5. $4\,139\,775 \div 135$

6. $62\,096\,895 \div 621$
7. $217\,753\,536 \div 1056$
8. $468\,086\,949 \div 1333$
9. $4\,510\,615\,818 \div 4567$
10. $518\,495\,670 \div 345$

11. $141\,271\,148\,922 \div 6551$
12. $78\,504\,370\,736 \div 248$

C

Find the remainders when these are divided.

1. $12\,352 \div 24$
2. $53\,461 \div 164$
3. $157\,572 \div 306$
4. $430\,673 \div 2044$

5. $944\,944 \div 499$
6. $1\,056\,844 \div 1045$
7. $2\,622\,222 \div 6222$
8. $31\,485\,044 \div 1555$

9. $1\,763\,856\,859 \div 7758$
10. $9\,999\,999\,999 \div 9999$

D

For each one, write out and answer the division or multiplication sum, then answer the question in words.

1. A *parsec* is a unit of distance used to describe the distance between stars and galaxies in astronomy. It is equal to 29 310 624 000 000 km. Another unit is the *light-year*. This is the distance travelled by a photon of light in one year. To find the size of a light-year, multiply a parsec by 10 (easy!) and then divide by 31.

2. Divide a light-year by 365 to find the size of a light-day.

3. Find the size of a light-hour.

4. Find the size of a light-minute.

5. Find the size of a light-second.

6. There are 1 000 000 000 *nanoseconds* in one second. Work out how far light travels in a nanosecond.

7. The light from the Sun takes 8 minutes and 17 seconds to reach us. Work out how far we are from the Sun.

8. Proxima Centauri, the nearest star to the Sun, is 1570 light-days from us. How far is this?

9. The highest speed achieved by a spacecraft is 160 800 km per hour, by one of NASA's *Voyager* probes. How long would it take to reach Proxima Centauri at this speed?

> Note:
> time = distance ÷ speed

10. *Pioneer 10* is currently the furthest human-made object from the Sun. It is now 9 600 000 000 km away. Radio waves travel at the speed of light: how long would it take a radio signal to reach *Pioneer* now?

Think for yourself ...

Six Sixes

(a) How many different divisions can you make, just using six sixes and some division signs?
Examples: 66 666 ÷ 6 = 11 111; 6666 ÷ 66 = 101.
Ignore any remainders when working out the answers. The answers must be bigger than 0, i.e. 1 or higher.

(b) Try this with five fives.
Are there more or less different divisions than you found for six sixes?
Why do you think this is?

(c) Try four fours, three threes, etc.

(d) What about larger numbers?

Division 9

Dividing by multiples of ten

Keywords ● divide ● place ● column ● zero

A

Feed these numbers into the ÷ **10** machine. Copy the table and fill in the output column.

	Input numbers	Machine	Output numbers
1.	50, 70, 90, 110, 130		
2.	2500, 3500, 4500, 5500, 6500		
3.	9100, 8700, 8300, 7900, 7500	÷ 10	
4.	1020, 1040, 1060, 1080, 1100		
5.	236 000, 347 000, 458 000, 569 000, 680 000		
6.	145 200, 167 400, 189 600, 211 800, 234 000		

B

Feed these numbers into the ÷ **100** machine. Copy the table and fill in the output column.

	Input numbers	Machine	Output numbers
1.	1400, 1200, 1000, 800, 600		
2.	5300, 4300, 3300, 2300, 1300		
3.	71 000, 67 000, 63 000, 59 000, 55 000	÷ 100	
4.	426 000, 537 000, 648 000, 759 000, 870 000		
5.	155 300, 177 500, 199 700, 221 900, 244 100		

C

Find the missing numbers in these calculations.

1. 500 ÷ ? = 5
2. 170 ÷ ? = 17
3. 260 ÷ ? = 26
4. ? ÷ 100 = 18

5. ? ÷ 10 = 221
6. ? ÷ 100 = 206
7. 1800 ÷ ? = 18
8. 84 300 ÷ ? = 843

9. 1030 ÷ ? = 103
10. ? ÷ 10 = 6800
11. ? ÷ 10 = 3060
12. ? ÷ 100 = 35 000

D

Use what you know about removing zeroes to make these easier to answer.

1. 4000 ÷ 20
2. 5500 ÷ 50
3. 6000 ÷ 300
4. 28 000 ÷ 700

5. 16 000 ÷ 40
6. 40 000 ÷ 800
7. 120 000 ÷ 600
8. 3500 ÷ 70

9. 36 000 ÷ 90
10. 225 000 ÷ 300
11. 34 300 ÷ 700
12. 420 000 ÷ 60

E

Feed these numbers into the function machines. Copy the table and fill in the output column.

	Input numbers	Machine	Output numbers
1.	5000, 7000, 9000, 11 000, 13 000	÷ 1000	
2.	550 000, 450 000, 350 000, 250 000, 150 000		
3.	5 020 000, 4 040 000, 3 060 000, 2 080 000, 1 100 000	÷ 10 000	
4.	92 000 000, 84 000 000, 86 000 000, 78 000 000, 70 000 000		
5.	145 000 000, 167 000 000, 189 000 000, 211 000 000, 234 000 000	÷ 1 000 000	
6.	7 000 000 000, 16 000 000 000, 25 000 000 000, 34 000 000 000, 43 000 000 000		

Think for yourself...

More Powerful Tens

(a) Copy this line:
100 (2 zeroes) = 1000 (3 zeroes) ÷ 10 (1 zero).
(b) Now write at least **three** similar lines starting with 100 (2 zeroes).
(c) Now write **three** lines starting with 1 000, and **three** lines starting with 10 000.
(d) Carry on this pattern, each time writing **at least three** lines starting with the same number.
(e) Is there a rule which describes what you have found? Test it out using some really *big* numbers.
(f) What happens if you split a number so that there are **three** numbers being divided to make it?

Factors

Keywords ● divide ● divisible ● factor ● multiple ● prime ● composite ● square

A

You can use your knowledge of multiples to answer these questions:

1. Is 2 a factor of 36?
2. Is 3 a factor of 36?
3. Is 5 a factor of 21?
4. Is 10 a factor of 230?
5. Is 6 a factor of 15?
6. Is 9 a factor of 45?
7. Is 4 a factor of 222?

8. Is 7 a factor of 56?
9. Is 8 a factor of 56?
10. Is 12 a factor of 132?
11. Is 11 a factor of 132?
12. Is 15 a factor of 235?
13. Is 20 a factor of 150?
14. Is 100 a factor of 400?

15. Is 18 a factor of 198?
16. Is 16 a factor of 92?
17. Is 25 a factor of 375?
18. Is 30 a factor of 370?
19. Is 50 a factor of 600?
20. Is 60 a factor of 600?

B

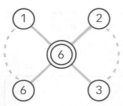

This is a factor diagram for the number **6**.

Notice how the factors appear in pairs.

Some numbers, like **7**, only have two factors – 1 and the number itself. These numbers are called **prime**. A number like 6, that has more than two factors, is called **composite**.

During this exercise, you will find some numbers that seem to have an "odd" factor that doesn't pair up with anything, like **25**.

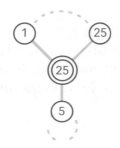

These are called **square** numbers. The answer to the puzzle is that the "odd" factor pairs up with *itself*.

Now, starting at **1** and working your way up, draw factor diagrams for as many numbers as you can – aim to reach **50** at least.

C

Find the missing factors from these lists. The factors have been written in order of size. You could draw factor diagrams to help.

1. **86:** {1, ?, 43, ?}
2. **75:** {1, ?, 5, ?, 25, 75}
3. **96:** {1, 2, ?, 4, ?, ?, 12, 16, ?, 32, ?, 96}
4. **78:** {1, ?, ?, 6, ?, ?, 39, 78}
5. **102:** {1, 2, ?, 6, ?, 34, ?, ?}
6. **152:** {?, 2, 4, ?, ?, 38, ?, 152}
7. **124:** {1, 2, ?, 31, ?, ?}

8. **366:** {1, ?, 3, ?, 61, ?, 183, ?}
9. **495:** {?, 3, ?, 9, 11, ?, 33, ?, 55, ?, 165, 495}
10. **180:** {1, ?, 3, ?, ?, 6, ?, 10, 12, ?, ?, 20, ?, 36, 45, ?, 90, ?}
11. **666:** {1, 2, 3, 6, ?, 18, ?, 74, ?, ?, ?, 666}
12. **1070:** {1, ?, ?, ?, ?, 214, ?, 1070}

D

Find **all** the factors of these numbers (The number in brackets tells you how many there are).

1. 95 (4)
2. 100 (9)
3. 64 (7)
4. 72 (12)
5. 140 (12)
6. 360 (24)
7. 250 (8)
8. 432 (20)

E

Sometimes, two numbers have some of the same factors. These are called **common factors**. The largest of these is called the **highest common factor**, or **HCF** for short.
Example: 20 and 30.

Factors of 20:   {1, 2, 4, 5, 10, 20}.
Factors of 30:   {1, 2, 3, 5, 10, 15, 30}.

Common factors: {1, 2, 5, 10}.
HCF = 10.

For each set of numbers, make a list of the common factors, then write down the HCF.

1. 8 and 12
2. 15 and 18
3. 26 and 39
4. 45 and 48
5. 32 and 60
6. 42 and 70
7. 60 and 80
8. 75 and 225
9. 6, 12 and 15
10. 15, 35 and 60
11. 16, 24 and 56
12. 24, 48 and 84

Think for yourself ...

Factor Quest

(a) Find the two-digit number that has the greatest number of factors.
(b) Find the three-digit number that has the greatest number of factors.
(c) Find the pair of two-digit numbers that have the greatest HCF.
(d) Think of some more puzzles like these.

Mixed Operations 1

Adding and subtracting

Keywords ● add ● subtract ● sign ● group ● collect ● digit

A

Find the answers to these. You should work through like this.
Example: 25 + 12 − 4 − 17.

$$25 + 12 = 37.$$
$$37 − 4 = 33.$$
$$33 − 17 = \textbf{16}.$$

1. 16 + 8 − 13
2. 64 + 17 − 75
3. 39 − 20 + 55
4. 166 + 46 − 105

5. 495 + 495 −166
6. 323 − 32 − 100
7. 1660 − 425 + 1212
8. 777 + 3077 − 34

9. 2500 − 617 − 517
10. 32 650 − 12 005 + 1025
11. 14 000 + 3 160 − 10 201
12. 4532 − 1450 + 20 663

B

Here are lots of number machines. Each has a letter.

A	+ 10	B	− 9	C	+ 5	D	− 12
E	− 99	F	− 30	G	+ 321	H	+ 125
I	− 120	J	+ 451	K	+ 75	L	− 733
M	− 603	N	+ 24	O	+ 1	P	− 4
Q	− 1000	R	+ 1010	S	− 400	T	+ 2500

Starting with each number given, use the correct machines in order to find the answer.
Example: 20, 30, 40: **ABC** gives

$$20 + 10 − 9 + 5 = 46,$$
$$30 + 10 − 9 + 5 = 56,$$
$$40 + 10 − 9 + 5 = 66.$$

1. 10, 20, 30, 40: **COD**
2. 1000, 2000, 3000, 4000: **FISH**
3. 1000, 2000, 3000, 4000: **BATTER**
4. 10, 20, 30, 40: **CHIP**
5. 601, 611, 621, 631: **PEAS**
6. 4050, 4250, 4450, 4650: **MELON**
7. 15 000, 16 420, 17 840, 19 260: **QAQAQ**
8. 1690, 1580, 1470, 1360: **JIG**
9. 100 000, 130 000, 160 000, 190 000: **AMBROSIA**
10. 51 630, 52 540, 53 450, 54 360: **BLOODNOK**

C

Put in the + or − signs that make these statements true.

1. 5 * 4 * 6 = 7
2. 16 * 25 * 41 = 0
3. 100 * 14 * 21 = 65
4. 541 * 145 * 415 = 271
5. 18 * 7 * 11 = 22
6. 205 * 152 * 512 = 565
7. 699 * 199 * 399 = 101
8. 1050 * 255 * 505 = 1810
9. 1164 * 453 * 1234 = 383
10. 1414 * 707 * 606 = 101
11. 10 000 * 5177 * 4288 = 9111
12. 654 321 * 87 654 * 1234 = 565 433

D

You can simplify things by "grouping" your additions and subtractions together.
    Example: 300: **FINGER** means 300 − 30 − 120 + 24 + 321 − 99 + 1010.
Add up all the numbers being added (including the starting number):
    300 + 24 + 321 + 1010 = 1655.
Add up all the numbers being subtracted:
    30 + 120 + 99 = 249.
Take this away from the first total: 1655 − 249 = 1406, the answer to the question.

1. 535: **SIP**
2. 440: **PANS**
3. 1500: **CABBAGE**
4. 3345: **MESSAGE**
5. 761: **FASHION**
6. 1061: **AMBASSADOR**
7. 25 000: **CHRONICLE**
8. 16 500: **STATIONS**
9. 3526: **MISSISSIPPI**
10. 9550: **JANITOR**
11. 11 000: **PENTAGON**
12. 1212: **ENSNARED**

Think for yourself …

Countdowns

(a) How many different numbers can you make using the digits 321 in order, if you are allowed to use a + or − sign anywhere?
    Examples: 32 − 1 = 31; 3 + 21 = 24.
(b) What happens with shorter Countdowns (like 21, etc.)?
(c) What happens with longer ones (like 4321, etc.)?
(d) Is it possible to use Countups instead?

Mixed Operations 2

Mixing types of operations

Keywords ● add ● subtract ● multiply ● divide ● operation ● order ● precedence

A

Find the answers to these.

1. (a) $5 + 1 \times 6$ (b) $5 \times 1 + 6$
2. (a) $12 - 4 \div 2$ (b) $12 \div 4 - 2$
3. (a) $15 - 3 \times 3$ (b) $15 \times 3 - 3$
4. (a) $20 \div 4 + 2$ (b) $20 \div 2 + 4$
5. (a) $36 \times 2 + 5$ (b) $36 + 2 \times 5$
6. (a) $50 \div 10 - 5$ (b) $50 - 10 \div 5$

7. (a) $24 + 6 \div 3$ (b) $24 \div 6 + 3$
8. (a) $120 \div 12 + 4$ (b) $120 - 12 \div 4$
9. (a) $41 \times 6 + 25$ (b) $41 + 6 \times 25$
10. (a) $226 - 30 \times 4$ (b) $226 \times 30 - 4$
11. (a) $1500 \div 30 + 15$ (b) $1500 + 30 \div 15$
12. (a) $698 \div 2 - 2$ (b) $698 - 2 \div 2$

B

Be careful with these: think about whether your answer is sensible.

1. $4 \times 2 \times 2$
2. $9 \div 3 \div 3$
3. (a) $21 \times 2 \times 3$ (b) $21 \times 3 \times 2$
4. (a) $50 \div 2 \div 5$ (b) $50 \div 5 \div 2$
5. (a) $15 \times 3 \div 5$ (b) $15 \div 3 \times 5$

6. (a) $24 \div 3 \times 6$ (b) $24 \times 3 \div 6$
7. (a) $132 \times 4 \div 11$ (b) $132 \div 11 \div 4$
8. (a) $288 \times 2 \div 12$ (b) $288 \times 12 \div 2$
9. (a) $60 \times 4 \div 3 \div 5$ (b) $60 \div 4 \times 3 \times 5$
10. (a) $105 \times 5 \div 7 \div 3$ (b) $105 \div 5 \times 7 \times 3$

C

Insert the correct signs so that each statement is true.
Warning! There are *four* possibilities for *each* part of number 8. Can you find all of them?

1. (a) $2 * 5 * 6 = 32$ (b) $2 * 5 * 6 = 4$ (c) $2 * 5 * 6 = 16$
2. (a) $16 * 4 * 2 = 2$ (b) $16 * 4 * 2 = 14$ (c) $16 * 4 * 2 = 6$
3. (a) $21 * 5 * 5 = 21$ (b) $21 * 5 * 5 = 20$ (c) $21 * 5 * 5 = 22$
4. (a) $140 * 7 * 2 = 18$ (b) $140 * 7 * 2 = 978$ (c) $140 * 7 * 2 = 40$
5. (a) $33 * 3 * 11 = 9$ (b) $33 * 3 * 11 = 121$ (c) $33 * 3 * 11 = 0$
6. (a) $15 * 6 * 2 = 180$ (b) $15 * 6 * 2 = 27$ (c) $15 * 6 * 2 = 12$
7. (a) $120 * 10 * 2 = 140$ (b) $120 * 10 * 2 = 14$ (c) $120 * 10 * 2 = 100$
8. (a) $2 * 1 * 1 = 1$ (b) $2 * 1 * 1 = 2$ (c) $2 * 1 * 1 = 3$

D

Find the answers to these: be careful with the order in which you work things out.

1. (a) $1 \times 2 + 6 \times 4$ (b) $1 + 2 \times 6 + 4$
2. (a) $4 + 5 \times 3 + 10$ (b) $4 \times 5 + 3 \times 10$
3. (a) $98 \div 14 + 7 \div 1$ (b) $98 + 14 \div 7 + 1$
4. (a) $100 \div 20 - 4 \div 2$ (b) $100 - 20 \div 4 - 2$
5. (a) $13 \times 6 + 5 \times 5$ (b) $13 + 6 \times 5 + 5$
6. (a) $750 - 20 \times 31 - 16$ (b) $750 \times 20 - 31 \times 16$
7. (a) $144 \div 4 \times 6 \div 3$ (b) $144 \times 4 \div 6 \times 3$
8. (a) $250 - 50 \div 10 - 5$ (b) $250 \div 50 - 10 \div 5$

E

Copy the grid and fill in the missing numbers.

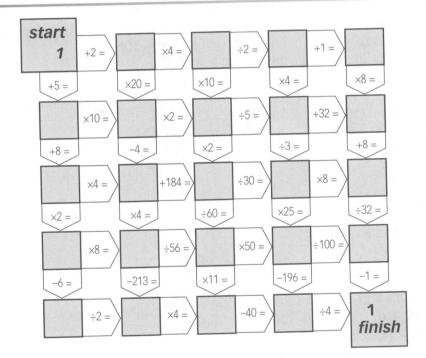

Think for yourself ...

Three's Company

Given any three numbers (for example, 1, 2 and 3), how many different answers can you make, using them in any order, and placing any sign you wish between them?
Example: $1 + 3 - 2 = 2$; $3 + 2 \times 1 = 5$, etc.

Brackets

Keywords ● order ● precedence ● open ● close ● nest

A

Answer these carefully. Each part contains the same numbers and operations, but with the brackets in different positions.

1. (a) $(9 + 4) - (3 + 5)$ (b) $9 + (4 - 3) + 5$
2. (a) $(3 + 12) - (4 + 2)$ (b) $3 + (12 - 4) + 2$
3. (a) $19 + (41 - 3) + 25$ (b) $(19 + 41) - (3 + 25)$
4. (a) $(115 - 40) + (39 - 35)$ (b) $115 - (40 + 39) - 35$
5. (a) $21 - (4 + 6) - 5$ (b) $(21 - 4) + (6 - 5)$
6. (a) $200 - (10 + 60) - 50$ (b) $(200 - 10) + (60 - 50)$
7. (a) $(9 \times 4) \div (2 \times 3)$ (b) $9 \times (4 \div 2) \times 3$
8. (a) $2 \times (10 \div 5) \times 4$ (b) $(2 \times 10) \div (5 \times 4)$
9. (a) $(32 \div 4) \times (2 \div 2)$ (b) $32 \div (4 \times 2) \div 2$
10. (a) $(1250 \div 25) \times (10 \div 5)$ (b) $1250 \div (25 \times 10) \div 5$
11. (a) $(91 \times 10) \div (2 \times 7)$ (b) $91 \times (10 \div 2) \times 7$
12. (a) $2400 \div (8 \times 10) \div 2$ (b) $(240 \div 8) \times (10 \div 2)$

B

Do the same with these.

1. (a) $(2 + 5) \times (4 + 6)$ (b) $2 + (5 \times 4) + 6$
2. (a) $(121 - 6) \times (16 - 11)$ (b) $121 - (6 \times 16) - 11$
3. (a) $(6 + 9) \div (3 + 2)$ (b) $6 + (9 \div 3) + 2$
4. (a) $(55 - 25) \div (5 - 2)$ (b) $55 - (25 \div 5) - 2$
5. (a) $(4 \times 13) + (12 \times 5)$ (b) $4 \times (13 + 12) \times 5$
6. (a) $(10 \times 10) - (9 \times 9)$ (b) $10 \times (10 - 9) \times 9$
7. (a) $(420 \div 10) + (4 \div 2)$ (b) $420 \div (10 + 4) \div 2$
8. (a) $(150 \div 15) - (10 \div 5)$ (b) $150 \div (15 - 10) \div 5$
9. (a) $(2250 \div 15) - (10 \times 3)$ (b) $2250 \div (15 - 10) \times 3$
10. (a) $(20 \times 6) + (12 \div 4)$ (b) $20 \times (6 + 12) \div 4$
11. (a) $(144 - 72) \div (6 + 18)$ (b) $144 - (72 \div 6) + 18$
12. (a) $(88 + 12) \times (10 - 8)$ (b) $88 + (12 \times 10) - 8$

C

Place brackets in these to make them correct.

1. $1 + 4 \times 2 = 10$
2. $12 \div 6 - 2 = 3$
3. $85 + 10 \div 5 = 19$
4. $6 \times 8 - 2 = 36$
5. (a) $2 + 4 \times 5 - 3 = 27$　　　(b) $2 + 4 \times 5 - 3 = 10$
6. (a) $10 - 6 \times 5 + 2 = 28$　　(b) $10 - 6 \times 5 + 2 = 22$
7. (a) $10 \times 4 + 6 \times 8 = 88$　(b) $10 \times 4 + 6 \times 8 = 800$
8. (a) $10 + 6 \div 2 + 6 = 14$　　(b) $10 + 6 \div 2 + 6 = 19$　　(c) $10 + 6 \div 2 + 6 = 2$
9. (a) $80 - 8 \div 4 + 20 = 98$　(b) $80 - 8 \div 4 + 20 = 38$　(c) $80 - 8 \div 4 + 20 = 3$
10. (a) $32 + 4 \times 6 - 3 \times 12 - 10 = 10$
　　(b) $32 + 4 \times 6 - 3 \times 12 - 10 = 166$
　　(c) $32 + 4 \times 6 - 3 \times 12 - 10 = 210$

D

You can use brackets within brackets. To make it easier to see where one set ends and another begins, different shapes are used: ( ), then [ ], then { }, then ( ).
Find the values of these.

1. $[10 - (2 + 4)] \times 3$
2. $210 \div [(10 + 35) \div 3]$
3. $[(6 + 4) \times (13 - 9)] \div (2 \times 5)$
4. $\{[(10 - 10) \times 10] + 10\} \times 10$
5. $[150 \div (15 - 10)] \times [2 \times (1 + 4)]$
6. $\{[(9 - 1) \times 2 + 4] \div 10 + 3\} \div 5$
7. $200 \div \{80 + 4 \times [15 - 2 \times (89 - 84)]\}$
8. $[500 - (20 + 60)] \div [(60 - 46) \times 3]$
9. $\{[(10 + 10) \times 10] - 10\} \times 10$
10. $\{[(1 + 1)]\}$
11. $1\ 000\ 000 - \{[(99 \times 100) + 99] \times 100 + 99\}$
12. $(\{[[(1 + 1) \div 1 + 1] \div 1 + 1\} + 1) \div 1 + 1$

Think for yourself…

Four Fours

Using just four "4"s and any signs and brackets you like, try to make as many different answers as you can. Can you make all the numbers from 1 to 20?
You will need to use the square root ($\sqrt{\ }$) sign. $\sqrt{4} = 2$. Also, if you get stuck, your teacher will have another suggestion for you that may help.

Mixed Operations 4

Single-stage problems

Keywords ● operation ● identify ● words ● working ● altogether ● total ● left

A

1. Ann has 25 CDs and Becky has 13. How many do they have between them?
2. The first volume of an encyclopaedia has 520 pages, and the second volume has 488. How many pages does the whole encyclopaedia have?
3. Chris wants to record three programmes while he is out one evening. He has a blank 180-minute tape. The programmes are 95 minutes, 35 minutes and 45 minutes long. Can he fit them all onto his tape?
4. Vijay's computer has two hard disks. One is 80 megabytes and the other is 210 megabytes. How much storage does he have altogether?
5. Denise wrote four essays for her evening class this term. They had 2550 words, 1610 words, 3125 words and 2400 words. How many words did she write in total?
6. The Middleshire telephone directory has 21 577 business entries and 35 785 private entries. How many entries is that altogether?

B

1. A Supermarket started the day with 210 frozen pizzas in stock, and sold 93 during the day. How many were left?
2. A spacecraft weighs 550 tonnes on takeoff. It burns 310 tonnes of fuel, and drops two boosters that weigh 55 tonnes each. How much does the part of the spacecraft that reaches orbit weigh?
3. Albert's best score on *Alien Invaders* is 152 600. One day he makes an attempt to beat this but is 4750 points short. What was his score?
4. Jenny is trying to collect a set of 120 picture cards. She has 73 now. How many more does she need?
5. Sven's pay cheque for the month is for £675 after tax. He has to pay out £320 on essentials. What does he have left to spend?
6. An orchestra has 75 players. In one piece that they play, the string section (46 players) is not required. How many of them play the piece?

C

1. There are 24 baubles in a box of decorations. Stephanie buys 5 boxes. How many baubles has she bought?
2. Raoul eats a packet containing 16 mints every day. How many does he eat in a week?
3. There are 30 dozen eggs in a transport carton. How many eggs is that?
4. How many playing cards are there in 12 new decks?

5. A ream of paper is 500 sheets. There are 5 reams in a box. How many sheets is this?

6. Cherie shared out some sweets between eight people. Everyone got 21 sweets. How many were there altogether?

D

1. A ream of paper has to be divided up between the members of a class of 28. How many sheets will each get? How many spare sheets will be left over?

2. I think of a number, multiply it by 6 and get the answer 450. What was my number?

3. Andrew is putting out bread rolls on tables for a wedding reception. 160 places have been set. The rolls come in packs of 12. How many packs will he need?

4. A lottery win of £8 500 000 is divided between four winners. How much does each one receive?

5. Joan is putting party invitations into boxes. She starts with 2400 cards and fills 160 boxes. How many cards are in each box?

6. On his motorcycle trip through the United States, Garry found that he averaged 1500 km per week. How much is this each day, to the nearest kilometre?

E

1. Ronnie wanted to see if you get the same number of crisps in every bag, so he opened five bags and counted them. He counted 26, 23, 31, 24, 28, then ate them all! How many crisps did he eat?

2. There were 178 episodes of *Star Trek: The Next Generation* made, which was 99 more than *Star Trek: The Original Series*. How many *Original Series* episodes were made?

3. The Paragon cinema has 360 seats. How many tickets are sold for a film, if it fills the cinema every night for a fortnight?

4. Brian's disk can hold 1600 kilobytes. He has 741 kilobytes stored on it now. How much free space is there on the disk?

5. Rosie is never ill. One year, she asks her form tutor how many "present" marks she has in the register. The answer is 390. How many weeks were in the school year?

6. Eddie loves drinking "Dr. Coker". Each month when he gets paid, he buys eleven six-packs. How many cans is that?

Think for yourself...

Your Turn! (1)

Try to construct some single-stage problems yourself. You could write each one on a small piece of paper and try them out on other members of the class, or your teacher could collect them together to make an exercise for the whole class.

Mixed Operations 5

Two-stage problems

Keywords • operations • order • working

A

To work out how many octaves there are on a keyboard, subtract 1 from the number of keys, then divide the result by 12. Find out how many octaves these keyboards have (some may have keys left over).

1. Home keyboard: 49 keys
2. Professional MIDI keyboard: 61 keys
3. Concert grand piano: 88 keys
4. Early Moog synthesizer: 37 keys
5. Studio master keyboard: 73 keys
6. Melodica: 25 keys

B

1. To convert pints to litres, multiply by 4, then divide by 7.
   Convert to litres:
   (a) 14 pints   (b) 70 pints   (c) 91 pints   (d) 350 pints
   Convert to pints:
   (a) 24 litres   (b) 16 litres   (c) 40 litres   (d) 120 litres
2. To convert miles to kilometres, multiply by 8, then divide by 5.
   Convert to kilometres:
   (a) 10 miles   (b) 30 miles   (c) 80 miles   (d) 110 miles
   Convert to miles:
   (a) 24 km   (b) 80 km   (c) 120 km   (d) 400 km
3. To convert kilograms to pounds, multiply by 11 and divide by 5.
   Convert to pounds:
   (a) 10 kg   (b) 25 kg   (c) 45 kg   (d) 90 kg
   Convert to kilograms:
   (a) 33 lb   (b) 66 lb   (c) 132 lb   (d) 2240 lb

C

Calculate the average speed on the following journeys.

Journey	Distance	Elapsed time	Rest/stop time
1.	50 km	90 mins	30 mins
2.	100 km	2 hours 30 mins	30 mins
3.	200 km	3 hours	1 hour
4.	540 km	7 hours	1 hour
5.	150 km	2 hours 45 mins	45 mins
6.	750 km	10 hours	2 hours 30 mins

D

Holton's Builders work 8-hour days. How many hours will they need to bill their customers for on the following jobs?

1. 3 full days and 2 hours
2. 5 full days and 6 hours
3. 12 full days and 3 hours
4. 20 full days and 4 hours
5. 11 full days, then a break, then another 4 full days
6. 1 full day and 5 hours
7. 10 full days and 4 hours
8. 50 full days, then a break, then another 12 full days
9. 124 full days, then a break, then another 16 full days and 2 hours
10. Four separate jobs that took 2 full days each

Think for yourself …

Your Turn! (II)

Try to construct some two-stage problems yourself. You could write each one on a small piece of paper and try them out on other members of the class, or your teacher could collect them together to make an exercise for the whole class.

Three-stage problems

Keywords • operations • order • working

A

Here are some number machines.

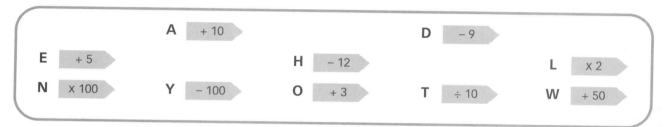

Use the right machines in the right order to answer the questions.

1. 200 → **THE** → ?
2. 4 → **END** → ?
3. 99 → **OLD** → ?
4. 12 → **HAT** → ?
5. 7 → **NEW** → ?
6. 150 → **TON** → ?
7. 15 → **LOW** → ?
8. 400 → **WHY** → ?
9. 6000 → **TOY** → ?
10. 3 → **NOD** → ?

B

Find the numbers that were fed in.

1. ? → **DOT** → 2
2. ? → **LEA** → 25
3. ? → **TAN** → 1400
4. ? → **WAY** → 513
5. ? → **EAT** → 10
6. ? → **ATE** → 15
7. ? → **ONE** → 1005
8. ? → **TWO** → 28
9. ? → **LAW** → 116
10. ? → **HAY** → 4501

C

To convert a temperature in degrees Celsius (°C) to degrees Fahrenheit (°F), multiply by 9, divide by 5, then add 32. Convert these to °F.

1. 50 °C
2. 100 °C
3. 25 °C
4. 180 °C
5. 450 °C
6. 700 °C

Convert these to °C.

7. 320 °F
8. 32 °F
9. 95 °F
10. 590 °F
11. 86 °F
12. 1112 °F

D

To work out the areas of these quadrilaterals, add together the "heights" of the triangles, multiply by the length of the horizontal line, then divide by 2. All measurements are in cm, but the drawings are not to scale.

1.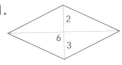

2.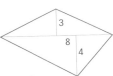

3.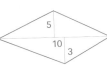

4.

5.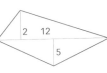

6.

7.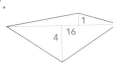

9.

8.

10.

Think for yourself…

Territory

Question: If all the land in the world were divided equally between all the people in the world, how much space would each of us have? Lots? Enough? Very little? Use the information given below to try and find an answer.

There are approximately 6 billion people on the Earth.
The diameter of the Earth is 12 746 km.
The surface area of a sphere is given (approximately) by 3 × diameter × diameter.
¼ of the Earth's surface is land.
¼ of this area is uninhabitable.

Supplementary (hard) question: if we each had the same amount of space, how far away would the next person be, on average?

Three-stage problems (tree type)

Keywords ● comparison ● total ● difference

A

Tickets for the Funworld theme park cost £8 for adults and £5 for children. Tickets for The Amazing Adventure cost £12 and £4. Find the cost of sending these different groups to each park, and say which one works out cheaper.

1. 2 adults and 3 children.
2. 4 adults and 4 children.
3. 2 adults and 25 children.
4. 4 adults and 81 children.

5. 10 adults and 155 children.
6. Which park would you recommend for **(a)** families, **(b)** school trips?

°B

Copy and complete the tables using the given number machines.

	Input 1	Input 2	A	B	Output
1.	3	7			
2.	15	15			
3.	70	13			
4.	2	99			
5.	100	100			
6.	644	5			

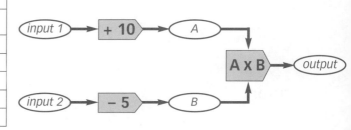

C

Copy and complete the tables using the given number machines.

	Input 1	Input 2	A	B	Output
1.	100	7			
2.	50	5			
3.	610	10			
4.	84	6			
5.	240	3			
6.	1075	18			

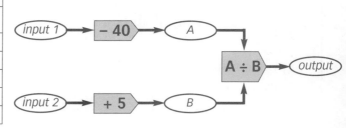

D

Employees at the Hawksvale car factory work a basic 38 hour week, and are paid overtime at double time.
For each of these employees, work out their basic pay, their overtime pay and their total pay for the week.

1. Andy earns £6/hour and did 4 hours overtime.
2. Tom earns £6/hour and did 10 hours overtime.
3. Aditya earns £7/hour and did 4 hours overtime.
4. Lloyd earns £7/hour and did 2 hours overtime.
5. Donald earns £12/hour and did 1 hours overtime.
6. Susan earns £9/hour and did 7 hours overtime.
7. Julie earns £4/hour and did 2 hours overtime.
8. Danielle earns £4/hour and did 5 hours overtime.
9. Gina earns £5/hour and did 7 hours overtime.
10. Chris earns £2/hour and did 3 hours overtime.

E

InterStar Rail offers these discounts for block bookings:
20–50 seats, *£1 per passenger*;   20–100 seats, *£2 per passenger*;   over 100 seats, *£3 per passenger*.
Work out the cost of these bookings on InterStar:

1. 15 seats at £12 each.
2. 25 seats at £10 each.
3. 36 seats at £20 each.
4. 67 seats at £4 each.
5. 150 seats at £25 each.
6. 205 seats at £16 each.

Think for yourself...

Cuboids

A **cuboid** (rectangular box) has three measurements – width, length and height. To work out the **volume** of the box, multiply these three things together. To work out its **surface area**, you need to open the box out into its **net**. You will get six rectangles, arranged in three pairs (top/bottom, front/back, left/right). Adding up the areas of all the rectangles gives you the surface area.
Given the information that a box has a volume of 200 cm^3,
(a) Find all the possible sizes for the box (e.g. 2 cm by 10 cm by 10 cm);
(b) find which one of these has the smallest surface area (the one in part (a) is 240 cm^2).
(c) Try the same thing with a box whose volume is 640 cm^3.
(d) Now try it with 800 cm^3. Can you come to any conclusions about the cuboid that has the smallest surface area?

Organising and displaying information

Keywords ● bar chart ● line graph ● pie chart ● order ● table ● chart ● organise

A

Year 9 at Fairport School did a survey of all the eye colours in their maths classes. These are the results.

9T: blue 11, brown 12, green 3, grey 1, hazel 2. **9A**: brown 11, blue 14, green 1, grey 2.
9R: hazel 2, blue 9, brown 16. **9G**: green 3, blue 13, hazel 1, brown 8.
9E: brown 9, blue 13. **9I**: blue 9, brown 10, grey 2.
9N: grey 1, blue 6, hazel 1, brown 8. **9U**: blue 5, grey 1, brown 4, green 2.

1. Organise the information.
2. Draw a graph or chart to show the numbers of pupils in the Year 9 maths classes.
3. Draw a graph or chart to show the numbers of pupils in Year 9 with different eye colours.

B

Danielle plays in an orchestra. She is interested in seeing how the orchestra is divided up into its different sections. She makes a list of how many people play each instrument.

1. Organise the information.
2. Draw a graph or chart to show how the instruments are divided up between the sections. Danielle uses *Woodwind*, *Brass*, *Strings*, *Percussion* and *Others*.
3. Do the same for the types of instrument in the *String* section.

bass drum, 1	oboe, 3
bassoon, 3	piano, 1
cello, 8	second violin, 10
clarinet, 3	snare drum, 1
cymbals, 1	tambourine, 1
double bass, 4	timpani, 1
first violin, 12	trombone, 3
flute, 3	trumpet, 4
glockenspiel, 1	tuba, 1
harp, 1	viola, 6
horn, 4	

C

These figures tell you the number of inches of rainfall recorded each month in two different cities.
January: Bombay, 0; Tokyo, 2. **February**: Bombay, 0; Tokyo, 3. **March**: Bombay, 0; Tokyo, 4.
April: Bombay, 0; Tokyo, 4. **May**: Bombay, 1; Tokyo, 5. **June**: Bombay, 20; Tokyo, 6.
July: Bombay, 24; Tokyo, 5. **August**: Bombay, 15; Tokyo, 5. **September**: Bombay, 10; Tokyo, 9.
October: Bombay, 3; Tokyo, 7. **November**: Bombay, 1; Tokyo, 4. **December**: Bombay, 0; Tokyo, 2.

1. Organise the information.
2. Draw a graph or chart to illustrate this information.
3. Comment on how useful your work is for comparing rainfall in the two cities.

D

Here are some figures from when Andy was ill, over a two–week period. His temperature (in °F) and pulse rate (in beats/min) are given.
Monday: first week, 98, 62; second week, 100, 95.
Tuesday: first week, 98, 65; second week, 101, 91.
Wednesday: first week, 99, 70; second week, 99, 84.
Thursday: first week, 100, 80; second week, 100, 78.
Friday: first week, 101, 83; second week, 99, 75.
Saturday: first week, 102, 90; second week, 98, 72.
Sunday: first week, 102, 94; second week, 98, 65.

1. Organise the information.
2. Draw a graph or chart to show how his temperature changed during the two weeks he was ill.
3. Do the same thing with his pulse rate.
4. Could these two things be shown on the same graph or chart?

Think for yourself ...

Find the Connection

It is sometimes said that people who are good at science are also good at maths. Here are the test scores for one set of pupils who took the same maths and science tests.

Robert: maths 13, science 14. **Angela**: maths 9, science 12. **Steven**: maths 16, science 15. **Jaspal**: maths 11, science 11. **Dean**: maths 12, science 10. **Alan**: maths 18, science 20. **Sarah**: maths 19, science 20. **Rachel**: maths 14, science 13. **Monica**: maths 10, science 12. **Joey**: maths 8, science 5. **Chandler**: maths 12, science 9. **Phoebe**: maths 15, science 16. **Ross**: maths 20, science 18. **Susan**: maths 19, science 18. **Michael**: maths 6, science 8. **Zack**: maths 9, science 9. **Lyta**: maths 17, science 15. **Mira**: maths 17, science 18. **John**: maths 15, science 14. **Leonard**: maths 14, science 14.

Organise the information in a helpful way, then think about how you could investigate whether people who are good at science are also good at maths.

Money problems

Keywords ● pounds ● pence ● cost ● discount ● income ● expenditure

A

Find the change each of these customers gets from the corner shop.

1.	John		4 batteries		20p each		£1
2.	Terri		3 comics		80p each		£5
3.	Don		12 pork pies		45p each		£10
4.	Adrienne		5 kg potatoes		21p per kg		£2
5.	Mavis	buys	6 soft drinks	costing	35p each	and gives the shopkeeper	£20
6.	Dick		4 pens		£1.40		£6
7.	Rochelle		1.5 lb cheese		£2.16 per lb		£5
8.	Wendy		3 bottles of milk		42p per bottle		£1.50
9.	Stanley		2 magazines		£3.75 each		£10
10.	Winston		15 bags of crisps		22p each		£3.50

B

Shirley is looking at evening classes and is trying to decide which three to do, but wants to get good value for money. Work out what these classes cost per week, and decide which will be cheapest for her.

Get Fit for Summer!   6 weeks, £24
Making Paper Decorations   10 weeks, £45
Word Processing   8 weeks, £56
Family History   12 weeks, £42
Aerobics for Beginners   8 weeks, £24
D.I.Y. Techniques and Tips   9 weeks, £28.80
Listen to Music   12 weeks, £18
Learn to Line Dance   8 weeks, £28
Painting Still Life   10 weeks, £41
Indian Cookery   8 weeks, £34

C

Flintbury School mathematics department has got the go-ahead to buy a complete new set of maths text books for all its pupils.

There is a single book for Year 7, another for Year 8, then the books they use for Year 9 come in three types: Extension or "E" books for maths sets 9F and 9L, Main or "M" books for sets 9N, 9T and 9B, and Core or "C" books for sets 9R and 9Y. This pattern continues into Years 10 and 11.

You will need to see a copy of the **Price list** (on a separate sheet or overhead projector).

Here is a breakdown of the maths sets at Flintbury.

	Year	7	8	9	10	11
Set	F	27	28	31	30	31
	L	28	28	30	30	29
	N	27	27	28	29	29
	T	26	26	27	28	27
	B	26	27	25	26	27
	R	27	26	21	20	23
	Y	27	26	15	14	15

They are going to buy the right text book for each pupil, one answer book for each class, and one resource book for each year.

1. Work out what this will cost.
2. What is the average cost per pupil?

Think for yourself ...

Maths Books in Your School

If you can find out how many pupils there are in each maths group at your school, you could work out how much it would cost to buy new maths text books for yourselves. You may be able to get hold of a price list for the actual mathematics scheme you use. If not, use the one on the **Price list** sheet.

Mixed Operations 10

Measures problems

Keywords ● length ● mass ● capacity

A

How many 15-cm lengths of string can I cut from pieces this long:

1. 50 cm?   **2.** 1 metre?   **3.** 2 m?   **4.** 5 m?   **5.** 10 m?

How many 6-inch lengths can I cut from pieces this long:

6. 2 feet?   **7.** 3 ft?   **8.** 5 yards?   **9.** 10 yd?   **10.** 20 yd?

B

These are the ingredients for Zeera Murgh, a spicy chicken dish, to serve 6 people.

2400 g chicken pieces   12 cm^3 fresh ginger
60 ml lemon juice   3 tsp cumin seeds
24 g plain flour   300 ml plain yogurt
48 g butter   150 ml double cream
180 g chopped onions   to taste: salt, cayenne
3 cloves garlic   pepper, lemon rind

In addition, 600 g Basmati rice should be cooked to accompany the chicken.

1. Work out the amount of ingredients necessary for one person.
2. Write the list of ingredients needed to cook this dish for 4 people.

C

Work out which package is the best value for money.

	Product	First package amount	First package price	Second package amount	Second package price
1.	wholemeal flour	500 g	54p	250 g	30p
2.	shower gel	50 cl	£1.50	20 cl	70p
3.	plaster	5 kg	£8.99	8 kg	£13.50
4.	lemonade	2 l	£1	3 l	£1.40
5.	car hire	2 days	£70	5 days	£145
6.	petrol	30 l	£20.70	25 l	£16.25

D

To find the density of a substance in kg/m³, divide the mass in grams by the volume in cm³, then multiply by 1000.
Use the information below to work out the density of the substances involved.

1. A small aluminium plate 10 cm by 10 cm and 1 cm thick has a mass of 270 g.
2. 5 kg of copper is made into a block 3 cm by 11 cm by 17 cm.
3. A 1 m² window is 5 mm thick and weighs 13 kg.
4. A gold bar is 5 cm by 5 cm by 25 cm. Four of the bars weigh 50 kg.
5. 1 litre of water weighs 1 kg.
6. A pint of methylated spirit (568 ml) has a mass of 454 g.
7. Half a tonne of anthracite occupies 270 000 cm³.
8. The enamel on a bath is 2 m² in area and 1 mm thick, and weighs 5 kg.
9. When I fill my car up with 50 litres of petrol, it gets 36 kg heavier.
10. A room 3 m by 5 m by 8 m contains 120 kg of air.

Think for yourself...

Wet, Wet, Wet

Work out the mass of water in these.
(a) A small swimming pool (shallow end 1 m deep, deep end 2 m, length 25 m, width 15 m).
(b) A full-size Olympic pool (2 m deep, 50 m long, 25 m wide).
(c) A lake (use sensible dimensions, perhaps a lake you know).
(d) The Earth's oceans (area of oceans × average depth, 3808 m). See 'Think for Yourself' in *Mixed Operations 6* for Earth data.